SIS Volume XIV, Number 3

Creating the Post-Communist Order

The Last Leninists
The Uncertain Future
of Asia's Communist States

by Robert A. Scalapino

foreword by Stephen Sestanovich

The Center for Strategic
and International Studies
Washington, D.C.

Library of Congress Cataloging-in-Publication Data

Scalapino, Robert A.
    The last Leninists : the uncertain future of Asia's Communist
states / Robert A. Scalapino : foreword by Stephen Sestanovich.
        p.   cm.—(Creating the post-communist order) (Significant
issues series, ISSN 0736-7136 ; v. 14, no. 3)
    Includes bibliographical references.
    ISBN 0-89206-191-X
    1. Communism—Asia. 2. Post-communism—Europe, Eastern.
3. Communism—China. 4. Communism—Korea (north).
5. Communism—Vietnam. 6. China—Politics and government.
7. Korea (North)—Politics and government. 8. Vietnam—Politics
and government. I. Title. II. Series.
HX376.A6S33 1992
335.43'095—dc20   92-10694
                                                                          CIP

Cover design by Hasten & Hunt Graphic Design, Inc.

Contents

About the Author

Robert A. Scalapino is Robson Research Professor of Government Emeritus at the University of California at Berkeley, where he founded and was director of the Institute of East Asian Studies from 1978 to 1990. He has been editor of *Asian Survey,* a scholarly publication, since 1962.

Professor Scalapino is a fellow of the American Academy of Arts and Sciences and has received research grants from the Guggenheim Foundation, the Social Science Research Council, and the National Endowment for the Humanities, among others. He was recently awarded the Order of Diplomatic Service Merit, Heung-In Medal by the government of Korea and the Order of the Sacred Treasure by the government of Japan. His extensive travels throughout Asia have included service as a visiting lecturer at Peking University in 1981 and 1985, as head of the U.S. delegation to the Second Mongolian International Conference in the fall of 1990, and as head of a U.S. mission on Korea sponsored by the Asia Society in 1991.

He has written several hundred articles and 36 books on Asian politics and U.S. Asian policy. His recent books include *Asia and the Road Ahead, The Foreign Policy of Modern Japan, The United States and Korea: Looking Ahead, Modern China and Its Revolutionary Process, Major Power Relations in Northeast Asia,* and *The Politics of Development: Perspectives on Twentieth-Century Asia.*

Professor Scalapino serves on the boards of Pacific Forum/CSIS, the Atlantic Council, the National Committee on U.S.-China Relations (of which he was a founder and first chairman), The Asia Foundation, and the Asia Society. He was recently named director emeritus of the Council on Foreign Relations.

Foreword

More than 30 years ago "world communism" was a term of common parlance, used to describe an international political movement held together, if not by central control, at least by shared outlook and purpose. The unity of the movement did not last, of course: the Chinese challenge to Soviet leadership made the term irrelevant. Scholars and policymakers gradually cast aside the image of a Communist monolith and began to learn the language of decentralization and diversity.

Now the study of world communism is back. In its new meaning, the term refers not to a global movement with common purposes but to political systems experiencing a common crisis. The year 1989 was marked by large popular demonstrations against one Communist regime after another, and the first and largest of these was organized not in Europe but in China. The huge rallies in Tiananmen Square were, and remain, the biggest expression of anti-Communist sentiment ever seen in the Communist world. Despite the bloody repression that followed, the meaning of the event seemed clear enough: communism's crisis was a single, worldwide phenomenon. Mikhail Gorbachev's visit to Beijing during the demonstrations, which seemed to embolden those calling for the ouster of his hosts, showed that the convulsions of European communism could not easily be confined to Europe itself.

Almost three years ago, the Center for Strategic and International Studies (CSIS) began an investigation of the growing pressures on Leninist systems around the world and of the new institutions appearing in their place. Under the title *Creating the Post-Communist Order,* our goal has been to understand the common features of the broad challenge to totalitarian regimes by exploring those cases in which the challenge has succeeded as well as those in which it has, so far, failed. The failures (or successes, from the current rulers' point of view) are Robert Scalapino's starting point in the present monograph, *The Last Leninists.* Looking at all the Communist states of East Asia, he asks whether the status quo can survive in any of them—and gives a strongly negative answer.

To many this answer may come as a surprise, for since the Tiananmen massacre European and Asian communism have seemingly traced very different courses. The Communist Party of the Soviet Union is now banned on its home territory. All the East European regimes founded by Joseph Stalin at the end of World War II have also disappeared, unable either to resist or to repress the Tiananmen-style crowds that formed outside their own gates. By contrast, the regimes founded by Mao Zedong, Ho Chi Minh, and Kim Il Sung are still standing (as is, for that matter, Kim himself). However often it is claimed that communism has collapsed, the fact remains that Communist parties count more than a billion people among their subjects.

Yet, despite the resilience of Asia's Leninist regimes, it is hard to read Scalapino's survey without recognizing the very forces that undid Soviet and East European communism. The political sclerosis created by aged and inflexible leaderships is much the same whether the ruler is named Honecker, Zhivkov, or Kim; the fact that the old man at the top (like János Kádár or Deng Xiaoping) has some reformist instincts of his own does not by itself solve the problem. The regimes of European communism were demoralized by a powerful demonstration effect that seems to be at work in Asia as well: Communist planners cannot match, but cannot ignore, the prosperity of their capitalist neighbors. Perhaps most important, the keepers of Communist power everywhere have had to contend with the emergence of what is commonly called "civil society"—social, political, and economic forces slowly escaping state control. In this connection, it is nothing short of astonishing that close to half of China's industrial output is already produced by non-state enterprises.

In Europe, Communist leaders reacted to these challenges with growing ideological confusion. Comparable incoherence is visible in Asia. The Chinese Politburo's declaration in March 1992 that whatever improves the people's material life is *ipso facto* "socialist" could easily have been authored by Aleksandr Yakovlev or Mikhail Gorbachev, the two main wreckers of Leninist thought in the Soviet Union.

Analysts of Asian communism sometimes argue that its leaders will be saved from European-style upheaval because, while they experiment with economic reform, they draw the line at political change. This *has* been true, and yet the first tentative signs of tinkering with political institutions are now visible: elections will be held in Vietnam in the fall of 1992, and proposals are being heard that the Chinese national legislature take on greater responsibility for forming the government. These are small changes, but it is worth recalling that experiments with partially free elections had catastrophic results for Communist rule in the Soviet Union and Eastern Europe.

From Robert Scalapino's careful study of the cracks in the Communist edifices of East Asia, it is clear that no single outcome is likely; local factors will continue to govern the political evolution of "world communism." Yet, in a larger sense, Scalapino foresees a common fate for all of Asia's Leninist rulers. Not only are the problems that they face the same ones that brought down communism in Europe, they are remarkably similar from one Asian country to another. By asserting these continuities, the author makes a powerful case that the status quo cannot endure.

The Center's project, *Creating the Post-Communist Order,* has been generously supported from the outset by the Lynde and Harry Bradley Foundation. We are glad to acknowledge that support again today.

Stephen Sestanovich
Director, Russian and Eurasian Studies
CSIS
April 1992

Introduction

The disintegration of the Soviet Union and the end of Leninism in Eastern Europe have amazed the world, but nowhere has the shock been greater than in the Leninist states of Asia. Once before, in the aftermath of the Twentieth Congress of the Soviet Communist Party in 1956, an ideological breach divided the Western and Eastern branches of the Marxist-Leninist community. That episode was costly to both sides, with the principal antagonists openly hurling epithets like "revisionist" and "national chauvinist" at each other.

In its pure form, however, the cleavage did not last long. The People's Republic of China (PRC), the nation that had led the charge against Nikita Khrushchev and his associates, managed to sully its own image during the Cultural Revolution, even with many Asian comrades. The Vietnam War brought the Soviet Union as well as China into powerful supportive roles on behalf of Hanoi. And by the 1980s, the Chinese leaders, now placing enhanced priorities on economic development, wanted to normalize relations with the Soviet Union to reduce the costs and risks of confrontation.

Even as this change in Sino-Soviet relations was taking place, however, new domestic conditions in both societies were under way. From the beginning, some aspects of the Gorbachevian reforms privately bothered leaders in Beijing, Pyongyang, and Hanoi. How far would *glasnost* go, and would it be contagious?

The Asian Leninist states did not have a legacy of a meaningful civil society apart from the state (such as a semi-independent church). They had not been contaminated by the pervasive influence of Western individualism. Moreover, unlike the East Europeans and various elements within the old Soviet empire, they did not need to reassert nationalist impulses against Russian domination. Hence, they did not experience the same pressures as their Western comrades for political reform. Further, they correctly questioned whether in the absence of effective economic reforms, political relaxation might not lead to chaos—the most dreaded condition for societies that had previously endured such a state for varying periods.

To be sure, the need for economic changes in the Western Leninist states could not be denied, least of all by the Chinese leaders, who had launched their own reform program more than five years earlier. Moreover, at first, they were somewhat reassured when Mikhail Gorbachev made it clear that he was a reformer, not a revolutionary; that he wanted to improve socialism, not overturn it.

At different points, the Asian Leninists' mood changed from apprehension to incredulity—and deep inner anger. For China, the transition was complex because even as the Soviet reformers began to lose control of the process of domestic change, steps toward Sino-Soviet normalization continued. Those steps were vital to both sides, and no one wanted them jeopardized by ideological polemics. Accommodation came in the form of public statements by Beijing that every nation was free to follow its own political path without external interference.

To the party faithful, however, Russia has been repeatedly held up as a powerful negative example in confidential documents. Developments in Eastern Europe and in the former Soviet Union have reinforced the determination of all current Asian Leninist leaders not to surrender a monopoly of power, whatever political alterations are made. Resentment of Gorbachevian policies, as we shall see, has been particularly bitter in North Korea. In Vietnam, the parting has been more amicable but no less painful.

What an extraordinary contrast with the situation prevailing at the birth of Asian communism, and the subsequent advent of the major Asian Leninist regimes, nearly a half-century ago. Then the Soviet Union was the symbol of the future to the young Asian Communists—an example of how to move from autocracy and backwardness to political and economic modernity within the life span of a single generation. And how the Asian Leninists wanted to make up for lost time!

In addition to an ideology of development, Leninism offered a science of organization to revolutionaries whose predecessors had repeatedly failed, and that was equally important. The advanced West had been both a threat and a disappointment, being imperialist on the one hand and offering models seemingly inapplicable to Asian circumstances on the other. To satisfy conditions in their real world, those Asians wanting drastic change had to connect the concept of "democracy" with mass mobilization, communalism, and—above all— unity. Democracy could not be allowed to stand for permissiveness, individualism, and diversity. The Leninist (mis)application of democracy fitted their needs.

In this connection, the issue of culture arises. The debate over whether culture is an important variable in explaining political difference or whether the emphasis should be on stage of development will never be wholly resolved. Moreover, it is a futile debate. Culture is an important factor, but it is not the sole factor. Societies strongly influenced by Confucianism (including Korea and Vietnam, as well as China) had a particular type of patriarchal communalism that influenced both values and policies. At the same time, societies that were pre-industrial and predominantly agrarian (with a mode of production involving elaborate irrigation systems and intensive manual labor) shared important characteristics influencing politics as well as other aspects of life.

Nor can one ignore the personal factor. Asia—traditional and modern—has had diverse types of leaders, some innovative, others deeply committed to preserving the status quo. This diversity has been very important, given the supremely important task of coming to terms with a West that after the eighteenth century (not before) was increasingly more "advanced." To lose years by attempting to stand still or to pursue erroneous policies was to waste a crucial commodity—time.

The timing of the emergence of "developing" societies in the past century has also been highly significant. Timing has determined the stage of the scientific-technological revolution at the point when these societies entered it, the models provided by other states that might be adapted, and the tempo of change possible—hence, the political as well as the economic alternatives available. In sum, communism, while far from inevitable, was a child of its times.

With these fundamental considerations in mind, I begin this study with a brief analysis of the specific factors that played important roles in the emergence of the Asian Leninist states. War, and notably global war, was a major stimulus, as had been the case with the advent of communism in Russia. Beyond ideological inspiration, moreover, how significant was Soviet material aid at the close of World War II? And how were the forces of nationalism and internationalism interwoven into the initial appeal of the Asian Communists? From whence came the early leadership, and how did those leaders relate to the "traditional" and "modern" forces that contended for influence both in their society and in their movement?

Next I turn to the Communist consolidation of power. One learns much about a political movement by observing carefully the manner in which it consolidates power after victory. Is it inclusive or exclusive? How is the newly obtained power distributed, and do means exist to check abuses of power? Violent political upheavals, however necessary in certain settings, involve waste. Individuals with education and experience are eliminated—lost as a resource. Moreover, an effort is often made to wipe the slate clean, to eradicate everything that is "old," replacing it with the "new." Yet this is not possible, and generally the attempt produces additional waste because those aspects of tradition that might be helpful to modernization are shunted aside while other, less helpful aspects remain in the interstices of the new system, adapting themselves to the changed environment by acquiring new forms and names. As will be noted, one of the most pervasive aspects of traditionalism to survive in the Asian Leninist states has been a pyramidal structure of power, narrowing at the top to a small group or a single individual.

The varied influences of tradition in the modernization process deserve serious reflection. The truly revolutionary societies of modern Asia—those where the pace of economic, social, and political change has been dizzying in recent decades—managed to make certain aspects of tradition serve the developmental cause while allowing or compelling other aspects to disappear. If one defines revolution not as a single political act but as a process of accelerating an ever more fundamental change, the creative use of tradition in this process is a vital element still little studied or understood.

Next, I turn to the core of the Leninist crisis. It is ironic that the "science" upon which Leninism was based, namely, Marxist economic determinism, has been instrumental in

Leninist decline. All of the Leninist societies of Asia sought to skip the capitalist stage, and now all are seeking to return to it in some degree. Of course, the present effort is labeled the creation of socialism with Chinese (Korean, Vietnamese) characteristics. Still, the attempt to raise the role of the market in the economic order is at the very center of the current reform efforts in China and Vietnam, and it is coming in North Korea. In each case, moreover, the critical issue is whether a command and a market economy can coexist in some fashion.

In their effort to use the state as an instrument of rapid development, the current Leninist leaders of Asia start not only from different philosophic principles but also with a structural situation different from that which confronted the leaders of modern Japan and those states we have labeled the newly industrializing economies (NIEs) when they began their post-1945 march. Thus, although many Leninists secretly admire the accomplishments of the neomercantilist market economies and hope to borrow some aspects of their system, barriers exist that are not easily overcome.

Drawing up a balance sheet on the current economic conditions of the Asian Leninist states is not easy. The situation is in constant flux, with a mixture of successes and failures and rapidly evolving policies aimed at correcting the most obvious deficiencies. Yet there is a reluctance to take the truly radical measures now under way in Russia and much of Eastern Europe—with the exception of Mongolia and Cambodia, two states whose current leaders openly proclaim that they are leaving Leninism. Asia's other Leninist leaders insist that they will find a way to advance socialism while taking into account their states' specific circumstances.

The outcome of that effort will obviously be crucial to the survival of each regime because performance, not faith, has become ever more crucial to the legitimacy of Leninist governments. Indeed, the present worry of the Asian socialist leaders—and not without reason—is that the earlier esprit de corps and idealism that marked the initial Communist phase are being swept away by crass materialism and its attendant ills. Their concern is that hedonism is becoming the order of the day, especially among younger generations corrupted by "bourgeois liberalism."

Because the verdict on the economic reform efforts is still out, one must be cautious in predicting the timing and the nature of political alterations in Asian Leninism. The pressures upon the prevailing order are strong and mounting. To resist these, one word dominates the official literature: *stability*. Leaders insist that without stability, no progress is possible in the economic or the social realm. In the most fundamental sense, they are correct; and this is a powerful weapon in their hands, especially in China, where even the intellectuals fear the type of chaos that prevailed during the Cultural Revolution. On the other hand, it must be asked whether the type of hard authoritarianism epitomized by the Leninist system is actually conducive to stability in the long term. It has not proven so in the West, and as events in Asia now demonstrate, the process of economic change itself threatens a political system that has limited capacity for adaptation. I indicate how the key Leninist governments are attempting to cope with this problem by using the traditional Asian technique of "listening to the voice of the people." In the penultimate section, I turn to the foreign policy issues confronting current Leninist leaders. In this revolutionary era, the interrelation between domestic and foreign policies has become ever closer, and fundamental questions relating to the concept of state sovereignty and the connections among the locality, the nation-state, the region, and the global system are emerging as supremely complex and pressing issues. It is especially difficult for the Asian Leninist states to handle these problems. On the one hand, they are committed to "turning out" for economic reasons. On the other hand, both because they harbor a recent legacy of imperialist threat and because they are still in the process of creating a nation, they cling to a nineteenth-century concept of the absolute sanctity of national sovereignty when the economic, political, and strategic trends make that view increasingly untenable.

It should be quickly added that their dilemma, although perhaps extreme, is by no means unique. The struggle among localism (often connected with ethnic or religious rivalries), nationalism, and internationalism is certain to be the most decisive contest of the coming decades. Moreover, it will encompass all peoples, irrespective of their economic and political systems.

I conclude by outlining four possible scenarios for the future of the Asian Leninist states. To posit an inevitable course—or a uniform course for each—would be unwise in my opinion. It is legitimate to suggest a table of probability, however, and this I have done. The one flat prediction that seems to me justified is that the status quo cannot survive. The changes ahead may be major, leading either to disintegration or to genuine political pluralism; they may be less drastic but real, leading to what I term "authoritarian pluralism"; or they may be very modest, leading to a reformed Leninism. But change is inevitable. Only its timing and extent remain to be determined. The revolution under way in the Leninist societies of Asia is not over; it has just begun.

1
The Background

Communism achieved power in parts of Asia in the aftermath of World War II. The war itself was a powerful catalyst. China's Kuomintang government was separated from the majority of its people for nearly a decade as a result of Japanese aggression. In the aftermath of "victory," moreover, Nationalist leaders were unable to cope with the massive problems of their society. A combination of serious Nationalist shortcomings relating to economic, political, and military policies and the Communists' organizational skills and ability to capitalize on mass dissatisfaction enabled the People's Liberation Army (PLA) to win the civil war in less than four years.

In North Korea also, the outcome of the war determined the course of politics. A Soviet army of occupation governed events, stopping at the 38th parallel in August 1945 through an agreement with the United States, whose military forces were not immediately available. Had no such agreement been reached, Korea would have been unified—under Soviet tutelage.

The conflict in Vietnam and the two other Indochina states of Cambodia and Laos was more protracted. Once again, however, World War II was a critical determinant of subsequent events. The Vietminh, which became the core of Communist strength, was born during that war, aimed first against the Japanese, then against the French, and finally—in different form—against the Americans. The immediate fate of the two smaller Indochina states was always contingent upon developments in Vietnam.

Communism in Mongolia had a different timing. Outer Mongolia was drawn into the Russian civil war in the years after 1917. When White Russians took control of Urga, the Mongolian capital, and used the region as a base for attacking the Reds, the Bolsheviks responded by driving them out. The Chinese, once rulers of Outer Mongolia, were racked by warlordism and unable to reassert their authority. Under Bolshevik nurturing and protection, a band of young Mongols

1

led by Sukhe Bator emerged, flying Communist banners and dedicated to independence from China. The final transformation took place in 1924. Sukhe Bator identified the Soviet role very frankly: "Our people is the internal force and the Soviet Union is the external support for the existence and flourishing of our Mongolian state. There is no other way for us."[1] With scarcely 1.5 million people sharing a border with the Chinese giant, there was indeed no other course if an existence separate from China was to be achieved then.

In the case of the other Asian Communist states as well, it is frequently asserted that in contrast to the situation in Eastern Europe, the Asian Communists were able to seize the nationalist issue, capitalizing upon the powerful anti-imperialist currents that were reaching high tide in the years after 1945. This view has merit, but several qualifications are in order.

First, nationalism was by no means a monopoly of the Communists; virtually every indigenous political movement in postwar Asia flew nationalist banners. Examples include the staunch defense of "the Chinese way" by Chiang Kai-shek and other Chinese Nationalists, the fiery nationalism replete with an undying hatred of the Japanese exhibited by Syngman Rhee, and the adamant rejection of the French (as well as his independence from the Americans) manifested by Ngo Dinh Diem.

Indeed, the Communists, in their commitment to a global proletarian brotherhood led by "the Great Soviet Union," proclaimed their internationalism more than did others. Was not the Soviet Union the motherland of socialism? The Communists did make effective use of anti-imperialist themes, directing their attacks variously against the Japanese during the war, the West Europeans whose colonial empires were breaking up, and the new global power, the United States. Nonetheless, they were not loath to acknowledge their indebtedness, both intellectually and later materially, to the USSR.

This acknowledgement signals another significant fact, namely, the importance of Soviet and, later, Chinese assistance to the triumph of communism in various Asian countries. Soviet aid in providing a Manchurian sanctuary and handing over captured Japanese military equipment to the Chinese Communists in the 1945–1947 period was probably not decisive in determining the outcome of the Chinese civil war, but it was certainly important. Moreover, despite the strenuous negotiations regarding assistance that took place during the Chinese-Soviet talks in Moscow after the Chinese Communist victory in the winter of 1949–1950, a badly wounded Soviet Union was very generous with the New China in the first years of Communist rule.

In turn, the victory of the Communists in China proved critically important to the Vietnamese Communist cause, opening up a route for the flow of military aid and making possible direct Chinese military support in such decisive battles as that of Dien Bien Phu. Indeed, the moral debt that Beijing felt the Vietnamese Communists owed it exacerbated Chinese bitterness at a later point. The Soviets also provided major logistical support to the Vietnamese Communists despite their own growing feud with the Chinese.

There is no need to dwell on the dependence of the Cambodian and Laotian Communist forces upon the Vietnamese, Chinese, and Soviets in the course of their rise to power, or that of the North Korean Communists upon the Soviets and, later, the Chinese. In all cases, Asian Communists were dependent, and often critically so, upon external sources of support. It is also true, of course, that those Asians opposing communism were at least equally dependent upon outside assistance, much of it coming from the United States after the onset of the cold war.

Another powerful factor abetting the Asian Communist cause was the appeal of an ideology that promised a way to combine political stability and rapid socioeconomic development while still paying homage to the central values of the modern world: democracy, social and economic justice, and the primacy of science and technology. One should not deny the idealism of many of the young Communist enthusiasts—and the overwhelming majority of them were young in 1945. They believed that they had the true vision of the future. They were certain that they had discovered the means to cast off the shackles of imperialist domination, to unify a disparate people, and to consummate a one-generation industrial revolution with social and economic justice for all.

With a few exceptions, the first-generation Communist leaders of Asia did not come from the traditional elite classes of their societies, but neither did they come from poor peasant or proletariat backgrounds. In the main, their antecedents were those of "middle" or "upper middle" economic strata, with an education well above that of the masses, although normally not sufficient to place them in the tiny minority of college graduates.

If one defines intellectuals in Asia in the pre-1945 era as those who had some higher education at secondary levels, not just college graduates, intellectuals have played a prominent role in the first-generation leadership of most Asian Communist movements, that of North Korea being a notable exception. Indeed, in the opening years of the Chinese Communist movement, the universities were often the spawning ground. Yet a number of early Asian Communists also had rural antecedents, reflective of the nature of their society. With few exceptions, however, they did not come from deep rural areas. Their native places were sufficiently close to urban centers to enable an acquaintance with new currents, including those from Japan and the West. Locales near urban centers also gave them access to higher education.

Those Asian Communist movements that achieved power, however, without exception went through a protracted guerrilla phase that strengthened their rural roots and also caused top positions to be shared with pure military-peasant types. The long struggle of the Chinese Communists from rural guerrilla bases after 1927 is well known. It was from this experience that the doctrine of using the countryside to surround the cities emanated. In the case of Korea, Kim Il Sung and his small Kapsan faction had operated from Manchurian bases until 1941, when they were driven into Siberia by the Japanese. The lengthy struggle of the Vietnamese Communists from jungle and mountain redoubts has been well publicized.

Irrespective of specific class origins, all successful Asian Communist leaders of the older generation were at some point revolutionary activists, accustomed to undertaking a broad range of functions. The lines between military and political activism are never sharply drawn in a revolutionary setting, nor are those between "administration" and such political tasks as mass mobilization. Thus, by definition, the first-generation Asian Communist revolutionaries were initially generalists. A division of labor was to come later. The strenuous, dangerous nature of their lives, moreover, bonded the survivors together in highly personal terms, with seniority a key to determining hierarchy.

In each of the Asian Leninist states, in contrast to the situation in most of their Western counterparts, the first generation—or its remnants—were still holding the pinnacles of power as the decade of the 1990s opened. Perhaps it is not surprising that they have retained the determination to maintain the faith that shaped their youth, whatever the adversities. The perceptions of an omnipresent bureaucracy and a dullness of life that are spreading among younger generations rarely penetrate their consciousnesses. They remain true believers.

At the same time, although they have spent a lifetime railing against the traditional order of their society, in many respects they remain a part of it and unable to escape fully the consequences of that fact. Indeed, the major Leninist modifications of Marxism were appealing to them in very considerable degree because those concepts were attuned to backward societies. Leninism used traditionalism in key ways even while denigrating it. The first-generation Asian Communists were and are Leninists more than Marxists, and their regimes should be known by that appellation.

Communism came to Asia when much of that vast region was in a pre-industrial and largely pre-urban stage, with huge peasant populations. Although there were large and medium-sized cities, the majority of urban residents had strong rural ties. The task of urbanizing Asian communism has been a prodigious one. Even while they were constructing industrial plants using the Soviet model, the first leaders had a mind-set deeply suspicious of much that was urban and modern. Thus, the move from an aging, somewhat xenophobic generation with rural guerrilla antecedents to better-educated, more technocratically oriented, cosmopolitan elites symbolizes a transition that will have an incalculable effect upon the future of communism, Asian-style.

2
The Consolidation of Power

The first order after the Asian Leninists achieved victory was to consolidate their power. This consolidation often resulted in the ruthless treatment of political opponents and those who belonged to socially and economically privileged classes. The number of individuals killed, imprisoned, or economically and socially "leveled" in the initial years after 1949 in the People's Republic of China will never be accurately known, but by most accounts it was high. The toll in rural areas was particularly heavy, with "oppressive" landlords or those defined as "petty tyrants" often dispatched by peasants acting as vigilantes. Urban capitalists generally escaped harm if they were not labeled Kuomintang lackeys and agreed to serve in their expropriated factories.[1]

Within the party, Mao Zedong's leadership had been firmly established after the "Rectification Campaign" of 1941–1942, but a few suspected rivals like Gao Gang were eliminated in the first years of the regime. By the late 1950s, however, serious cleavages threatened, the product of Mao's idiosyncratic policies and the spectacular failures that ensued. The stage was set for the Great Proletarian Cultural Revolution, a disaster that was to influence Chinese politics and economics profoundly in the post-Mao era. As late as 1971, Mao was to be challenged by a man whom he had called his "closest comrade in arms," Lin Piao, in a move indicative of the bizarre politics that took place in the imperial court that had been constructed around an aging emperor.[2]

The consolidation of power by the Korean Workers' Party—and Kim Il Sung—was more complex. At the outset of their occupation of Korea, the Soviets, recognizing the limited appeal, indeed, the limited existence of Korean Communists, established a government headed by a staunch Christian nationalist, Cho Man Sik. Military power, however, quickly gravitated into the hands of the minuscule Communist band headed by Kim Il Sung, who had become a Soviet protégé after

his sojourn in Siberia. Thus, when Cho defied Soviet authorities over an Allied plan for Korean trusteeship in the winter of
1945–1946, his removal and the ascendancy of Kim to power
were not difficult.[3]

It took many years, however, for Kim to obtain unchal–
lengeable authority. First, he had the leader of the South
Korean Communists, Pak Hon Yong, executed during the
Korean War. Later, in 1956–1957, he purged rivals from the
so-called Soviet and Yenan factions of the Korean Workers'
Party. It was during this period that Kim discovered the value
of nationalism as a weapon against domestic opponents. The
primacy of *chuch'e* (self-reliance) was established at this point.
Meanwhile, large numbers of Christians, former landowners,
and others of the upper classes had fled to the South in two
waves—shortly after Communist accession to power and
during the Korean War.

The consolidation of Communist power in Vietnam also
occurred in stages. Long before military victory over the
South, the Communist-dominated Vietminh had done battle
with assorted rivals from Trotskyites to various religious and
nationalist elements.[4] The terms of the Geneva Agreement of
1954 permitted repatriation of those wishing to move to either
the South or the North. More than 1 million Vietnamese, most
of them Catholics, went south. A much smaller number of
Communist supporters went north.

From this point, the Vietnam Workers' Party maintained
unity reasonably well, preoccupied as it was with the struggle
to take over the South. It also operated under a more collectiv-
ist leadership than other Leninist systems, a product of Ho Chi
Minh's style. Nonetheless, the evidence later given by defectors
and knowledgeable individuals suggests that inner party factionalism was continuous, some of it connected with differences over policies, much of it derived from the type of
personal-regional attachment or "tribalism" characteristic of
Asian societies.[5]

The events in Cambodia following the acquisition of power
by the Khmer Rouge (KR) have been widely publicized. There,
in the hands of French-trained radicals, Asian Leninist
fanaticism operated in its purest form. After the slaughter of

countless individuals considered to have been a part of the socioeconomic elite, including a large number of intellectuals, the new leaders denuded Phnom Penh and other cities, sending their citizenry into the countryside to become agrarian producers. Hundreds of thousands reportedly died of malnutrition, disease, and severe working conditions. The majority of rank-and-file Khmer Rouge soldiers displayed a primitivism that accorded with their youthfulness and harsh rural experience.[6]

The subsequent cleavages within the Khmer Rouge stemmed more from differences over international affiliations and high-level factional struggles than from disagreement over the initial genocidal policies. Truly, the revolution turned inward against a portion of its own. Only recently has the Hun Sen-Chea Sim government in Phnom Penh pledged a complete break with Leninism, as will later be discussed.

Laos, true to form, witnessed a less structured elimination of opponents. Most key figures of the previous era, Prince Souvannaphouma excepted, had fled the country, many settling in Thailand, others going to the United States or to France. Souvannaphouma, whose half-brother, Souvannavong, had long been a key figure in the Hanoi-affiliated Laotian Communist movement, the Pathet Lao, was given a conditional pardon by the new leaders and sank from sight in retirement. The monarch, living in Luang Prabang, was not so fortunate. He reportedly died while in detainment.[7]

It should be noted that several of the top leaders of the Pathet Lao had been connected with Vietnam in more than political terms: Kaysone Phomvihan, secretary general of the Lao People's Revolutionary Party (LPRP), is half-Vietnamese ethnically; Souvannavong's wife is Vietnamese; and there are others with similar ethnic ties. The principal problem for the Lao Communists has been with the Hmong, an ethnic minority, many of whom had been affiliated with General Van Pao's U.S.-sponsored anti-Communist forces. These elements, however, have never been regime-threatening.

In its consolidation of postvictory power and its own subsequent evolution, Asian Leninism has exhibited several significant structural traits. First, the pyramidal nature of the party sharpened, with supreme authority resting with a single individual, a figure increasingly unchallengeable. A cult of personality was fostered by all of the instruments of education and propaganda available, with those surrounding the "Great Man" playing leading roles.

China provides an excellent example of this phenomenon. By the time of the Cultural Revolution, which broke in its full fury between 1966 and 1969, Mao could ravage both the party and the government virtually at will, using the youthful Red Guards as his instruments. More astonishingly, this was possible despite the demonstrated failure of the commune system and the debacle of the Great Leap Forward, both of which bore his imprimatur. In the course of the Cultural Revolution, Mao toppled the great majority of his old comrades in arms, including some military men, and no one was able or willing to fight back. Zhou Enlai, one of the few key figures exempt from the purges because of his utility in keeping day-to-day affairs operating—and his long-demonstrated lack of will to struggle for supreme power—followed Mao passively despite his personal qualms. He had only marginal influence in softening the blows upon some colleagues.

With the overthrow of Hua Guofeng and the ascension of Deng Xiaoping to top authority in 1978, it became legitimate to criticize Mao, using a carefully crafted formula: "He was a great revolutionary and socialist, but in his later life, he made serious mistakes" (precisely the position taken by official Chinese sources on Stalin in the 1960s). Some attacks on Mao went much further, however, and his statue was removed from a number of places, including Peking University. An effort was made to dissociate the new government from a cult of personality. Yet, as we shall see, after the events of early 1989, culminating in the June 4 Tiananmen killings, Mao has again been elevated, with his collected works frequently cited as guides for thought and action.[8]

Unquestionably, the Democratic People's Republic of Korea (DPRK) has carried the adoration of the leader to its ultimate extreme. Not only the "Great Leader," Kim Il Sung, but the "Dear Leader," his son and designated successor, Kim Jong Il, and, indeed, the entire family back to the grandfather have been deified. Grandfather Kim is credited with having participated in the attack upon the U.S. warship *General Sherman* in

1866 when the vessel came to Korea looking for stranded U.S. seamen, thereby inaugurating the amazing exploits of this thoroughly revolutionary family.[9] Nothing symbolizes the extent to which the cult of personality has gone in the DPRK more than the fact that virtually all adults wear badges bearing Kim's picture when in public—a practice that was briefly encouraged in China when Mao's Cultural Revolution was at its height.

In Vietnam also, Ho Chi Minh's name has been increasingly invoked since his death in an effort to bolster the regime's legitimacy. Contrary to the attempt in North Korea to recreate an ancient sun god, omnipotent and omnipresent, Ho's heirs have portrayed their hero as a humble, unpretentious son of the soil, dedicated to the service of his people—Uncle Ho. Yet, he is buried in a mausoleum that is a precise replica of that holding Lenin (up to this point) in Moscow's Red Square. Moreover, this loyal servant of the Comintern has been anointed not merely Father of Country, but the patron saint of socialism, Vietnamese-style. "In accordance with Uncle Ho's prescription" precedes many contemporary instructions and admonitions.[10]

The different circumstances of Cambodian and Laotian communism have made charismatic leadership there less available, although that aura surrounds Salok Sar, alias Pol Pot, for his Khmer Rouge followers and no doubt would have been assiduously cultivated had the KR remained in power in Phnom Penh. In Laos, the position of Kaysone seems firm, although little effort has been made to create a special identity for him.

Much earlier, the Mongolian People's Republic (MPR) pursued a course similar to that in the principal Leninist societies of later times. Sukhe Bator, the short-lived "founder" of the MPR, died in 1923 at the age of 30; and throughout the early years, both before and after his death, there were many factional struggles and bloody purges. He was to be eulogized by all successors, however, and to have the central Ulaanbataar square named in his honor. Only in the past several years, with a very youthful Mongolian leadership having declared Leninism dead, has the cult of personality been banned.

It is not surprising that the struggle for power in elitist Communist circles was intense in virtually every case. In classic Leninism, all political institutions culminated in the party, and all power in the party culminated in the individual who emerged as supreme leader. The inner party struggle, moreover, was usually a zero-sum game, with the losers liquidated, politically if not physically. Hence, an atmosphere of fear was created, especially as the leader consolidated his position. In such an environment, frankness was risky, and knowing whom to join and when to retreat vitally important.

Political institutions other than the party had limited if any independence. In most cases, however, the top political elite held dual and even triple positions in the party, the government, and the military, thereby providing some degree of coordination. In all cases, law was subordinate to man. The judicial organs, such as they were, were neither independent nor given authority to apply the law in accordance with the judge's determination. Party edicts were supreme and evolved from the Standing Committee of the party Political Bureau, often from the determination of a single individual. Nonetheless, the system was soon conducive to the emergence of a massive and partially uncontrollable administrative bureaucracy. Orders from the top were frequently lost or diluted in the bureaucratic sea. It was this fact that caused a frustrated Khrushchev to remark, "How can I be a dictator? I can't even get the Moscow sewer workers to do their jobs effectively!"

More generally, the actual political situation under Leninism raises serious questions about the validity of the totalitarian model. Although critical decisions affecting the lives of all citizens were indeed the prerogative of a tiny elite, a great deal slipped through the cracks and crevices of this woefully inefficient system. Especially in continental-sized Leninist states, for millions of citizens, the emperor—and the party center—were far away, and local officials and cadres came in very diverse types.

Nonetheless, the crucial philosophical distinction between Marxism-Leninism and liberalism in political terms is that the Leninists believe in the perfectibility of a class (hence, of individuals); whereas liberals believe that there is a quotient of evil in all persons and hence that power must be limited. The consequences of that difference are difficult to exaggerate.

Leninism results in a government of men with their various frailties ultimately exposed but with the means of restraint exceedingly limited. Liberalism rests upon the supremacy of law, which serves to check the corruption of power.

3
The Economic Challenge

As the twentieth century moves toward a close, two powerful factors combine to make economic performance critically important to every state. First, the capacity of the scientific-technological revolution to produce rapid and dramatic changes in human livelihood and national power is now appreciated throughout the world. The level and health of a state's economy directly affect its capacity to play an effective role in the regional and global community. Indeed, power—the capacity to influence others—is determined increasingly by a nation's economic strength, with military power becoming a derivative and, to some extent, subsidiary element.

Second, the communications-information revolution that science has created has sharply reduced the ability of any government to keep its citizens isolated, hence, a captive audience to a single voice. Even in North Korea, a growing portion of the citizenry has heard about other countries from unofficial sources: returned students, visiting relatives who live abroad, workers dispatched overseas, and acquaintances among the military or diplomatic personnel stationed in foreign countries.

With knowledge of the outside, however distorted or partial, comparisons can be made. Increasingly, therefore, Leninist governments cannot achieve legitimacy merely on the basis of cradle-to-grave indoctrination; it must be earned through performance. The citizenry will no longer be satisfied with the collected works of Mao, Kim, or Ho. Now and in the future, they want material improvements like those taking place around them in the dynamic market economies of East Asia. Without exception, the current Leninist leaders of Asia are coming to recognize this fact and hence are attempting to pursue significant economic reforms even while recognizing that such a course carries political risks. It is appropriate, therefore, to explore the economic accomplishments and shortcomings of the Asian Leninist states at the outset and to examine the challenges that lie ahead.

The People's Republic of China

When the Chinese Communists came to power in 1949, they faced a truly formidable economic task. Half a billion people, many of them uprooted or impoverished by the recurrent violence of recent decades, faced a dire future. China suffered from the full range of economic problems: rampant inflation; dismantled or obsolete industrial plants; grave energy deficiencies; inadequate fertilizer, neglected water conservancy, and a shortage of other requirements for modern agriculture; a disrupted transport system; and a bankrupt treasury.

Measured against the staggering problems that were inherited, the PRC government's initial economic accomplishments were impressive. Within three years, inflation had been brought under control, industrial and agricultural production had been significantly increased, transport had been greatly improved in key areas, and foreign trade had expanded.

The creation of order throughout the nation under the most strongly centralized political-military system that China had ever known was one major factor enabling productive gains. In the agricultural realm, the initial program was "land to the tiller," a massive redistribution program that eliminated the old rural elite and accomplished Communist political control through village associations, cultivating local cadres at the same time as land reform was being effected. By the end of 1952, the new program was in operation.

There followed a campaign to promote cooperatives in which a group of families would form mutual aid teams, pooling labor and equipment. At first, there was considerable resistance to this step; but pressure was increased, and by the end of 1956 the cooperative movement covered some 90 percent of all rural households.

The radical experiment with People's Communes got under way in 1958. Administrative units the size of counties, comprising 5,000 to 8,000 households, were made the key source of decision making regarding production and allocation. Brigades and teams were created to undertake specific functions and were remunerated according to work points.[1]

In theory, the commune system was supposed to provide the basis for rural industrial development as well as the more effective management of large-scale irrigation and communications projects. The idea was to keep the peasant out of the cities by taking a self-sufficient economy to the rural areas and at the same time using the hitherto-underused peasant work force.

From the outset, evidence accumulated that the commune system had serious defects. Regimented peasants with a weak incentive system that skipped remuneration on the basis of the individual family's labor were not the basis upon which to build a work ethic. The communal kitchens were abandoned at an early point. Later, greater emphasis was placed on the team, but Mao and his associates stubbornly refused to recognize that the system would never promote the productive increases they sought.

The ill-fated Great Leap Forward was launched at the same time as the commune program in an effort to expand China's industrial base in record time. The labor force, urged on to new heights by ideological exhortation, was to substitute for machinery. The wholesale misuse of resources resulting from this naive effort (combined with several years of bad weather, which seriously reduced crop yields) created a first-rate disaster. According to some estimates, up to 20 million Chinese perished from starvation and malnutrition between 1959 and 1961. The parallel with Stalin's frenzied agrarian collectivization drive 30 years earlier was too clear to be missed.

Subsequently, the Great Leap was abandoned, changes were made in the commune system, and recovery ensued. The Cultural Revolution did not affect rural China extensively. Agricultural productivity throughout the period before 1980, however, was held back by low governmental investment, faltering modernization, and, above all, limited incentives for the farmer. The average increase in grain production was slightly over 2 percent per annum in the 1960s and 1970s, scarcely ahead of population growth.

It was in the industrial sector that the Chinese economy showed the major quantitative gains throughout much of this period. Nationalization had proceeded quickly; by 1956, all private enterprises had been incorporated into the new socialist order. Between 1952 and 1974, the average industrial growth rate was 10.5 percent, and this period encompassed two downturns, namely, in the early 1960s after the Great Leap failure and in the peak Cultural Revolution years between 1967 and 1969.

The Soviet model had been employed, albeit with certain modifications: centralized planning and control over key industries but with some degree of provincial and municipal authority over others; rigorous control over wages and prices, enabling large profits; and extensive investment directed at first primarily toward heavy industry. Producer goods were imported from China's socialist allies along with technical assistance.

By the late 1970s, however, serious problems were accumulating in the industrial as well as the agricultural sector. The ills of an autarkic economy now largely shut off from the Western socialist countries as well as the market economies were apparent to the discerning elements of the power elite. Agriculture, long neglected, was on a plateau from which it could not rise, and restiveness in many rural areas was manifesting itself in diverse ways. The industrial structure was badly out of balance, with energy, transport, and communications bottlenecks rife. Management inefficiency and low labor productivity were the unhealthy twins of the old system. Plant obsolescence had become an increasing problem with the most limited access to technologies that were changing with lightning speed.

Deng Xiaoping, at this point a veteran of many battles with the hard-shelled ideologues, sounded the call for reform with such famous phrases as "It doesn't matter whether a cat is black or white if it catches mice" and "Poverty is not socialism."[2] Following Deng's return to power, Deng's ideas and those of his associates were ratified by the Third Plenum of the Eleventh Chinese Communist Party (CCP) Central Committee meeting in December 1978.[3]

It is not surprising that one of the most spectacular of the reforms launched after 1978 was the abandonment of the commune in favor of the "family responsibility system," whereby individual families could contract for the use of land. In effect, this restored a form of private land operation, with the individual peasant family able to sell produce on the free market after delivering the contracted amount to the government.

In the industrial sector also, a degree of privatization was encouraged, with small-sized and medium-sized industries allowed to operate under individual or cooperative ownership. At the same time, a general "turning out" for foreign capital and technology was encouraged. To this end, Special Economic Zones (SEZs) were authorized, of which the most famous was Shenzhen, across the border from Hong Kong. In addition, decentralization of controls and authority, both authorized and unauthorized, got under way. Provinces and municipalities began to exercise greatly expanded power in collecting revenues, contracting loans (including foreign ones), and creating new enterprises and projects.

After 12 years, what type of balance sheet can be drawn up on China's massive reform efforts? On the positive side, aggregate growth has accelerated, averaging 8.8 percent for the post-1978 period. Most important, increases in overall agrarian productivity have averaged around 4 percent per annum, nearly double the pre-1979 rates. The dynamism of newly encouraged rural small-sized and medium-sized industries has been especially noteworthy and has contributed mightily to a rapidly rising rural income in many regions. With considerable justification, PRC authorities could claim at the beginning of the 1990s that the problems of food and clothing for the Chinese people had been basically resolved. Even the extensive floods of 1991 did not produce famine in the affected areas or food shortages in urban centers. Grain production for 1991 will be only slightly below the peak figure of 435 million tons if official projections are correct.[4]

Further, the pool of natural scientists and technicians has been greatly enlarged; in 1990, their numbers were reportedly 10.8 million. Through a variety of means, moreover, new technology has been acquired in certain important fields.[5]

There have been other positive developments. Since 1989, inflation has been kept under control, and the savings rate has been high, making money available for investment. The current public interest in the newly established Chinese stock exchange is one illustration. Private entrepreneurship, long quiescent under the socialist blanket, has reemerged and "rags to riches" stories circulate, sometimes inducing the "red-eye" disease (jealousy). Yet even Deng said that to get rich was all right—as an initial step toward mass affluence.

A major increase in the value of China's trade has also taken place; the 1990 total of U.S. $115.4 billion represented nearly a sixfold increase over the 1978 total. Indeed, some observers felt that the Chinese economy had become too dependent upon exports.[6]

On the negative side of the ledger, however, a formidable list of difficulties must be recorded.[7] Under any economic system, China would face stupendous problems. With 7 percent of the world's arable land, it contains 22 percent of the global population. Moreover, its 1.1 billion people are likely to reach 1.5 billion in the early twenty-first century despite the strict population control measures being attempted. In the past decade, the Chinese work force has increased by some 175 million, and an additional 92 million individuals will join the work force by the year 2000. Absorbing this work force will require that the target growth rate of 6 percent per annum be achieved or exceeded, and there will still be vast numbers of underemployed. Nor will the productivity gains be evenly distributed throughout the country, suggesting the likelihood of internal migration, possibly of troublesome proportions. Meanwhile, within a decade, large segments of the Chinese population will reach old age, rapidly requiring the creation of a social security system and significant alterations in the current generous retirement conditions.

Two fundamental problems remain unresolved by the reforms. First, PRC authorities have been unable or unwilling to control cyclical oscillations between ultrahigh growth fueled by credit expansion and steep contractions as inflation threatened to get out of hand. Second, China, like all Leninist societies past and present, has not yet come up with truly satisfactory answers to the central challenge of reconciling a command economy to a market economy. Both dilemmas warrant elaboration.

In the years since 1979, on three occasions the authorities felt it necessary to use fiscal and monetary policies to retard inflation, producing a "recession."[8] The worst cycle in this sequence took place between 1987 and 1990. In 1987–1988, stimulated by easy credit, industrial growth shot up, reaching 18 percent. Inflation got out of hand, however, rising to 27 percent officially and higher in urban centers. Moreover, when the government announced in mid-1988 that all price controls would be lifted the following year, panic buying ensued. The economic crisis induced deep political cleavages at the top of the Communist structure and contributed to the unrest in the spring of 1989 that led to the Tiananmen tragedy.

Beginning in the fall of 1988, the government resorted to drastic measures to bring the situation under control, tightening credit, cutting back sharply on construction and other expansionist activities, and retaining, even strengthening, price controls. The result was a sharp contraction of the economy, with growth shrinking to virtually zero by the fourth quarter of 1989. Inflation dropped precipitously, but so did sales. Unemployment rose, and urbanites in particular felt the pain of China's worst economic slump since the end of the Great Leap.

By 1991, the PRC had pulled out of the recession. The gross national product (GNP) increase over 1990 was 6 to 7 percent, with industrial production growing by some 10 percent. Significantly, town and township (rural) enterprise output accounted for between one-third and one-fourth of total industrial output. The present goal is "sustained, steady growth." Whether this goal can be achieved amid recurrent inflationary pressures remains to be seen.

Meanwhile, state-owned heavy and medium industry, epitomizing the "command" sector of the Chinese economy, is doing badly. In September 1991, the party felt it necessary to convene a special conference to discuss the problems.[9] According to official statistics, 36.7 percent of these enterprises were losing money. Triangular debt (purchasers not paying bills to plants that in turn cannot pay their debts to material suppliers) continues to mount. Moreover, many of the goods being produced by these industries are unwanted; by September 1991, items valued at some 200 billion yuan were stored in warehouses, a rise of 30 billion yuan over the same period one year earlier.

The poor performance of this sector is reducing state revenues because the government derives the bulk of its funds from these industries. Further, bailouts of failing enterprises are adding to governmental costs, causing "progressives" to argue that such firms should be closed, a view disputed by conservatives, who fear it would represent one more nail in the socialist coffin. Yet the budget deficit is substantial, and this problem is exacerbated because under the present revenue-sharing system, provincial and municipal governments get funds that previously accrued to the center.

Equally important, the different levels of performance within the industrial sector are lengthening the economic gap between China's backward regions (the Northeast and a portion of the Southwest, where large state-owned industrial plants dominate the scene) and the advanced regions (the Southeast, where collective and private enterprises, mainly light industrial and processing plants, are thriving). In this connection, a phenomenon is emerging that warrants careful attention. Natural Economic Territories (NETs) are being created between Guangdong Province, Hong Kong, and Taiwan, and also between Fujian Province and Taiwan. Cutting across political boundaries, these NETs raise highly significant issues of influence and control. Moreover, they are certain to grow. Southwest China has begun to look seriously at Southeast Asia. The troubled provinces of the Northeast long for closer economic ties with South Korea and Japan. In sum, vitally important parts of China are forming close economic attachments to neighboring regions, regions operating under very different economic and political systems.[10]

These developments raise a question perpetually faced by every continental-sized state: how much centralized control, how much decentralization? After the overthrow of the Manchu dynasty in 1911, China quickly fell into a tortured period of warlordism, with the center(s) scarcely able to exercise authority beyond their immediate regions—a cluster of provinces, a province, or sometimes only a city. Indeed, this problem plagued the Nationalists even after power was partially consolidated in 1927 and continued to do so until the victory of the Communists.

The Communists, as noted earlier, provided modern China with a greater degree of political unity and cohesion than it had previously known. After 1978, however, Beijing (before Moscow) came to accept the fact that a centralized, command economy could not function effectively in a country as vast and heterogeneous as China.[11] In this respect too, a certain pendulum-like swing has taken place. When unregulated credit at the provincial level soared, Beijing imposed fiscal and monetary controls. A two-tiered price system is maintained, with certain prices fixed by the center, others fluctuating with the market. Overall price deregulation continues to frighten authorities, who are aware of the inflationary results in the Western ex-Communist countries, including the Russian republic. Thus, although price reform has taken additional steps forward recently, including increases in house rents and the price of grain and edible oil, a portion of the economy operates on the basis of artificial prices, deterring efficiency. Structural imbalances also remain substantial. Energy, transport, and communications deficiencies retard advances to higher technology and the creation of a national market.

In addition, the absence of a public security system, plus the fact that for millions of workers the factory or organization provides a range of services from housing to child care and medical clinics, makes the implementation of new rules regarding labor difficult if not impossible to enforce. Despite injunctions that poor performers can be dismissed and the adoption of a new contract system for the 15 million workers in state-operated firms, the results thus far are minimal. The vast majority of workers cling to the "iron rice bowl," with too many hands for the work available, often doing too little and doing it inefficiently.

Meanwhile, an increasing number of rural underemployed and unemployed are traveling to the cities looking for work, despite the rapid growth of rural industries and overall improvements in rural livelihood. The need to take care of a huge new labor force lies ahead.

Finally, despite the pride exhibited in training a larger number of "scientists and technicians," the acknowledgment that science and technology will be a key factor in rapid progress, and recurrent assurances that intellectuals are truly respected, the economic remuneration—and the political treatment—given that group does not encourage entry into those fields. Many of the most highly trained—those who went to the West for their higher education—refuse to come home under present conditions. At the same time, the bureaucracy is so overstaffed that the government has pledged to trim its ranks along with cutting industrial and agricultural subsidies in an effort to bring down upward pressures on the budget.

Dai Yuanchen, a noted senior economist, most honestly summed up internal views of China's economic future at the beginning of 1991 when he said, "We are optimistic and worried."[12] He then extolled the progress made in the previous decade and foretold the dangers, ending with the injunction that China's best course lay in pushing market-oriented reform forward.

The dilemma is that certain policies implemented in the name of socialism for four decades, however uneconomic, underwrite social stability—massive subsidies, guaranteed employment, and the willingness to support permanently disabled state-operated enterprises among them. Others, including the pervasive bureaucratization of the society, with its attendant corruption in multiple forms, are inextricably connected with socialism.

The government is now looking toward a ten-year program and an eighth five-year plan. The aim is to develop what is called a "planned commodity economy"—in the vernacular, "socialism, Chinese-style." Premier Li Peng and others have put the broad guidelines as follows: the central task is economic growth; and the means, the "two basic points" of adhering to the Four Cardinal Principles (political Leninism) while pursuing domestic reform and an opening to the outside world in the economic realm. In this manner, China's current leaders hope to combine political stability and economic growth.[13]

Because pragmatism lies deeply imbedded in Chinese culture, together with a capacity to separate words and action, the ideologues may well lose their battle to retain the old system with only minor modifications. The changes already under way are too substantial to be reversed significantly or halted. The broad movement will probably be in the direction of a mixed economy, with privatization and decentralization growing hand in hand but with major state involvement continuing, both in planning and in ownership of certain economic sectors. The Japanese, South Korean, and Taiwanese models will continue to be studied without being precisely followed. The exact state-market mix will be subject to periodic shifts, with a linear progression unlikely. Yet the basic trend will be away from the Stalinist economic strategy, and the connections with the dynamic Pacific-Asian market economies will grow. This movement will include an accelerated quest for foreign investment, a quest with uncertain results given highly competitive international needs and the growing scarcity of available capital in the advanced industrial nations.

As noted, NETs will develop, involving portions of China, especially coastal China, with other economic-political systems. This development will constitute an additional risk for Leninism politically as well as economically—and possibly an additional strain on China's unity. In sum, China has only begun an economic journey down a long road with many uncertainties ahead. Only one prediction seems safe: an era featuring the centralized, command economic strategy is ending, and despite nostalgia in certain quarters and temporary retreats, it cannot be restored.

The Democratic People's Republic of Korea

When Kim Il Sung's Kapsan faction took power in early 1946, North Korea's dependence on the Soviet Union, economic as well as political, was overwhelming.[14] The North Koreans had inherited a heavy industrial base from the Japanese era; and it was relatively easy, with Soviet assistance, to adopt an orthodox Stalinist economic strategy. In addition to the emphasis on industrialization, the collectivization of agriculture was completed between 1955 and 1957. By the end of 1958, the private sector had virtually vanished; investment went primarily to the production of capital goods; and private consumption was slighted, with state-fixed prices to guarantee minimal subsistence.

Kim Il Sung's belief in the spring of 1950 that a strike at the South would enable rapid Korean unification proved to be

a disastrous miscalculation. The devastation of the North as a
result of that war required an almost complete rebuilding of
the DPRK economy. Generous assistance was forthcoming
from the USSR, with China and Eastern Europe also contribut-
ing funds and technology.

Growth rates from the late 1950s to the early 1970s were
high, and the North could boast that its economic development
was surpassing that of the South. Stalinist economics once
again demonstrated its "early sprint" capacity. North Korea's
extensive dependence upon both the Soviet Union and China
created serious problems, however, given the volatile nature of
developments within and between those two societies. When
Pyongyang sided with Beijing against Khrushchev "revisionism" in the late 1950s and early 1960s, Moscow retaliated by
cutting off economic cooperation until 1965, after the shift to
the Leonid Brezhnev-Alexei Kosygin leadership. During the
Cultural Revolution, relations with China worsened, and
Pyongyang again turned to the USSR.

The unpredictability of Communist bloc aid and its general
decline after 1961 (with no grant aid being given) led DPRK
leaders to look to advanced industrial societies for capital and
technology in the early 1970s. Both Japan and Western Europe
provided substantial loans, totaling some $1.6 billion. Most of
this money continued to be used to build heavy industries,
with agriculture and light industry slighted.

Then problems began to accumulate. North Korea's
autarkic economy and its lack of will to undertake structural
reforms limited its capacity to generate foreign exchange. The
first oil shock exacerbated the problems. Hence, it was unable
to repay the Western loans, or even the interest on them. With
North Korea's international credit rating very bad, once again,
in 1984, agreements were reached with the Soviets, Chinese,
and East Europeans to obtain advanced technology and military assistance. At the same time, in an effort to stimulate
investment, a joint venture law was enacted that September.

At this point, however, the North Korean economy was in
serious trouble. The goals set up in the Second Seven-Year
Plan (1978–1984) had not been reached. The North ceased
releasing statistics after 1965; but the evidence suggests that
after high growth in the early 1970s as a result of Western-

Japanese funds, a precipitous drop in growth occurred in the second half of that decade and continued in the 1980s. External investment came largely from pro-DPRK Koreans resident in Japan, and some observers considered it more a gift than an investment.[15]

Although no statistics relating to North Korea should be taken as indisputable, they do indicate basic trends with reasonable reliability. Informed analysts believe that growth between 1987 and 1990 did not exceed 1 to 3 percent and that GNP in 1990 declined 3.5 percent. Structural imbalances were rife. Serious energy shortages were made much worse by the economic collapse of the Soviet Union and the drastic curtailment of Soviet exports to the DPRK, together with a Soviet demand for hard currency transactions and international market rather than "friendship" prices.[16]

Some 50 percent of North Korea's trade, including the bulk of its oil, had come from the USSR. The Soviet Union, China, and Japan together had accounted for nearly 80 percent of its trade. By the beginning of the 1990s, two of these countries were ailing economically, and the Japanese private sector had the most limited interest in the DPRK economy, given its past experiences. With persistent trade deficits, North Korea had accumulated a debt of $6.8 billion by the end of the 1980s.[17]

North Korea's most fundamental problems were those of an autarkic system. They included the inability to operate on an economy of scale, technological obsolescence, serious energy and transport bottlenecks, and agricultural stagnation because of insufficient investment. Furthermore, there was a systemwide lack of incentives, with Stakhanovite methods used in their place, such as continuous "campaigns" organized as 100- or 200-day "struggles" aimed at increasing productivity—a method that has no lasting effect. Lack of competitiveness in the international market resulted in persistent trade deficits. To add to its woes, the North suffered bad harvests between 1988 and 1990 and had to import rice. Military expenditures, possibly totaling more than 20 percent of GNP, along with other extravagances, notably the costs of the World Youth Festival in 1989 and the numerous monuments erected in Pyongyang, were further economic burdens. Moreover, the so-called Taean management system employed in industry in

effect provided for collective management by party committees, a highly inefficient process.[18]

Privately, DPRK officials have acknowledged some of these
problems, and they are evident from an examination of the
Third Seven-Year Plan, proclaimed in 1987 and scheduled to
be completed in 1993. That plan set relatively low targets and
emphasized improving living standards, including increased
food production, light industry, and housing; using science and
technology to raise productivity, including the training of 2
million "technicians"; developing fuel and energy sources; and
expanding trade by 3.2 times. Reaching most of the goals set
forth in the plan is clearly impossible, given recent domestic
setbacks and the problems of those socialist or ex-socialist
societies upon which North Korea has been so dependent. Yet
they point the direction in which North Korean leaders have
recently sought to go.[19]

It would probably be a mistake to believe that the North is
on the verge of economic collapse. Its immediate economic
problems are more serious than those of China, and its reform
efforts are less advanced than those of either China or Vietnam. This is a disciplined society, however, and distribution to
the citizenry at large is rigorously controlled via rationing and
requiring coupons for most purchases. Inflation thus far has
been low. Naturally, the political elite live better, but conspicuous consumption by that quarter is discouraged. Scattered
reports on economic conditions from foreign residents visiting
relatives are generally strongly negative, with food scarcity
frequently reported. Life outside Pyongyang and one or two
other major cities appears to be far more rugged. Requests to
relatives for basic goods are frequent, and the very fact that
Japanese wives of repatriated Koreans are not allowed to visit
their homeland suggests concern about conditions being
reported. As of the early summer of 1991, however, the residents of Pyongyang and Wonsan did not give evidence of
malnutrition and were dressed simply but adequately.[20] In
sum, life in North Korea for the average citizen is spartan and
mobility is limited, but meagerness is more or less shared—
omitting the top leaders, of course. In addition, the ability of
the average citizen to make comparisons to life elsewhere is
still limited.

Nevertheless, using available statistics, comparisons between North and South Korea as of 1991 are dramatically unfavorable to the former. Various estimates placed the per capita GNP of the North in 1990 at between $1,064 and $1,500 per annum; that of the South was recorded at nearly $5,000. Because of heavy military expenditures, the North's private consumption was estimated at less than one-half of GNP in 1989, whereas in the South it was 65 percent. The difference in trade statistics in that same year is awesome: total trade for the North was $4.8 billion versus $118.2 billion for the South.[21]

Under these circumstances, it is not surprising that the North has shown increasing signs of undertaking the most substantial changes in its economic policies to date, changes that may go beyond the current plan. A younger, better-educated, somewhat more cosmopolitan generation is rising in the bureaucratic and party ranks under Kim Jung Il, the heir apparent. Sparse evidence indicates that at least some of these individuals recognize that past economic policies have reached a dead end and that efforts to alter them have been inadequate.

To what extent these people will have support from both the younger and the elder Kim is not clear, but some support must have been forthcoming to effect such alterations as have already begun. As early as 1984, peasant markets where items other than certain types of food, wine, and cigarettes could be sold began to operate openly; and recently these have reportedly expanded into regular, permanent marketplaces where surplus goods from cooperative farms and products of individual households are sold. In addition to food, these outlets offer used furniture, old clothing, and various other items. Thus, the basis for market expansion relating to the rural population exists.[22]

Meanwhile, because of its food emergency the North finally agreed in early 1991 to import 100,000 tons of rice from the South via a Korean-managed trading company operating from Japan and dealing directly with a South Korean firm. Indirect trade in other items surged upward in the same year, with the South exporting textiles, oil, and home electronic appliances in exchange for zinc, steel, and fishery products from the North.[23] At the same time, Pyongyang made it clear that normalization of relations with Japan had a high priority, with

economic considerations of obvious first importance.[24] Even
the periodic indications of a desire to improve relations with
the United States have economic as well as other motives.
With its traditional allies either undependable or not in an
economic position to meet DPRK needs, a turning out, however cautious, is under way. In 1991, an agreement was
reached with a Hong Kong-based restaurant chain operator to
establish the first joint venture bank in Pyongyang, with the
foreign entrepreneur holding a 51 percent stake.[25]

One must be cautious. There is as yet no indication that
chuch'e will be abandoned, at least as a central symbol of
socialism, Korean-style. In fact, however, the North was exces-
sively dependent upon either the USSR or China (or both)
under the old order. Now at least some of its leaders are envis-
aging growing relations with the market economies, including
that of the South. As noted, concrete plans for greatly expanded trade are being made. Some leaders in the North may
hope that this can be undertaken without the need for extensive domestic reforms, but this hope seems highly unrealistic.
To become competitive in the international marketplace, the
North will need to make major changes.[26]

Increasingly, DPRK leaders are studying the Chinese
experience, contemplating whether portions of it can be used.
Already, the idea of Special Economic Zones is being bor-
rowed, with discussions sponsored by the United Nations
Development Program (UNDP) of the Tumen River region or
possibly other sites getting under way, despite substantial
obstacles. The Chinese model is attractive to certain
Pyongyang leaders partly because it promises reform economically while holding the line politically. Even to get to the
Chinese position, however, will require a major change of
course. As yet, those in authority in the DPRK do not discuss
publicly the defects of their economy, unlike their compatriots
in China—and Vietnam.

Nevertheless, it can be predicted with reasonable confidence that the DPRK will undergo significant economic
changes, probably in the near future. Much depends upon
political developments, both at home and abroad. Some outside observers predict that after Kim Il Sung's death, the North
will rapidly disintegrate, going the way of East Germany.

Although this possibility cannot be ruled out, a more likely scenario is a combination of Deng's China and Park Chong Hee's South Korea, with or without Kim Jung Il, whether under military or civilian control (or a mixture). Whatever the precise economic route, although North Korea has a greater distance to go than the other Asian Leninist societies, a transformation is unavoidable in the near future.

Vietnam

The course of the Vietnam economy under communism has some resemblance to the path taken by China, but with significant differences. When the Communists won their war against the Thieu government in 1975 after U.S. abandonment of the South, they were determined to implant the Stalinist model throughout the country, despite its undistinguished performance in the North. The standard policies were enacted: a centralized, command economic structure was instituted, with supreme authority; heavy industry was emphasized, with other facets of the economy assigned lower priority in terms of investment; state-owned enterprises and collectives replaced private concerns; prices and wages were fixed; and agriculture was collectivized, although efforts were made to induce rather than coerce.

The task was complicated because the South had had some experience with a market economy, albeit under the artificial conditions imposed by extensive U.S. economic assistance and an all-encompassing war. Entering this scene, the Communists were determined to punish those who had been associated with the Vietnamese or U.S. enemy. Tens of thousands were sent to reeducation camps, including many whose training would have served the cause of economic rehabilitation. Others, including a number from the Chinese commercial community, had fled either at the time of Communist victory or shortly thereafter, frightened by the prospect of socialism, Hanoi-style.

The result was a disaster. Production, both agricultural and industrial, plummeted. Only bureaucratism—and corruption—flourished, as everyone, officials included, scrounged to survive. Peasants in the South, a great majority of whom had enjoyed private holdings after the Thieu land reforms, resisted the collectives. Factory workers, lacking incentives, labored in a plodding fashion.

New problems mounted in 1978–1979. Bad weather further reduced agricultural production, forcing massive importation of food. The decision to invade Cambodia to overthrow the Pol Pot government resulted in the imposition of economic sanctions by the West and led to a conflict with China. Soviet aid was reduced and rendered in the form of loans, not gifts.

With the reputation of the Vietnam Communist Party (CPV) and the Hanoi government falling to extremely low levels among the populace, the leaders decided to effect certain changes in the Third Five-Year Plan, launched in 1979. Under the label "New Economic Policy"—taking a leaf from Lenin's old book—the emphasis was placed upon improving livelihood by increasing the production of basic necessities, including food; promoting some decentralization, allocating more control to local units; and adjusting prices and wages to accord better with prevailing market conditions.

These measures, and particularly the permission granted to the agricultural cooperatives to sell surplus products on the free market and the increases in the government purchase price, resulted in greatly improved food supplies, although imports were still required. Small-scale industries producing consumer goods also advanced. Yet, in the absence of basic reforms, familiar problems mounted: government subsidies that served to keep prices low for necessities, together with the serious losses suffered by state-owned industries, resulted in growing budget deficits and rising inflation. In the midst of the surging economies of East Asia's NIEs and the promising advances of most members of the Association of Southeast Asian Nations (ASEAN), Vietnam had the unhappy distinction of being one of the world's poorest countries, with a per capita income of scarcely more than $200 per year.

Against this background, the Sixth Party Congress, held in December 1986, initiated an economic reform that came to be known as *doi moi* (renovation).[27] Party leaders now acknowledged that serious policy errors had been committed, and they signaled a more pragmatic approach, with a dedication to improving economic conditions. Premier Truong Chinh's

Political Report was overwhelmingly devoted to economic issues. Nguyen Van Linh, a Southerner, became the new general secretary of the party and, although shunning political liberalization, pledged himself to support economic reform rigorously. Do Muoi, a party elder regarded as a conservative, succeeded Truong Chinh as premier, suggesting a balance between party factions, but he too promised active support for the new program.

The commitment to improve agricultural production and consumer goods was reemphasized, and an export promotion program was espoused. A campaign to reduce the money supply and government deficit and to tackle inflation was announced. A strong interest was shown in attracting foreign investment, and subsequently various measures were enacted with this goal in mind. Further, as *doi moi* unfolded, farmers were given the right to withdraw from collectives; the contract term for those in collectives was extended; and individual farm families were permitted to lend or transfer land leased from such groups, thus shifting from socialist collectivism to what amounts to private ownership, akin to the Chinese model. In 1988, private corporations were authorized.

The initial developments after the congress were discouraging. Following dramatic price decontrols (for all items except electric power, water, gas, and transportation costs) inflation soared, reaching 700 percent annually in 1987. Structural imbalances, technological backwardness, and poor management continued to hobble industrial productivity. State-operated enterprises, holding some 85 percent of the nation's fixed capital assets, accounted for only 30 percent of the GNP. Moreover, as in China, the state enterprises busily produced goods no one wanted and hence were forced to consign such goods to storage or scrap. Domestic investment was meager. Further, a combination of economic conditions within Vietnam and the international embargo restrained foreign investors.

By the outset of 1989, however, *doi moi* seemed to be producing some gratifying results.[28] Inflation dropped precipitously to 30 percent that year, and rice production enabled Vietnam to be the world's third largest rice exporter. At least agricultural reform seemed to be working.

But by the end of 1990 it was clear that most other basic economic problems remained unresolved.[29] The inflation rate for 1991 was approximately 70 percent. Various factors were involved: the curtailment of trade and assistance from the Soviet Union and Eastern Europe—the same factors that plague the North Koreans; high fuel prices; weather-damaged crops; and tax evasion. Industrial production, both state and private, showed marginal increases or actual reductions, again in part because of the collapse of the old markets in Western socialist countries and the factors noted above. Natural disasters continued to hamper the economy, but despite bad weather and insect infestation in 1991, agricultural production was reasonably good. Nonetheless, state revenues, including remittances from abroad, were down. The nation suffered from massive unemployment, with some 1.7 million individuals jobless, most of them youth. With an additional 1 million individuals added to the work force yearly because of high birthrates, the task ahead is formidable. There is no sign of an adequate population planning program.[30]

Amidst these circumstances, the party held its Seventh Congress, June 23-27, 1991.[31] Prior to the congress, a number of articles and editorials appeared that were highly critical of or deeply concerned about prevailing conditions. One of the most interesting was by Pham Minh, who outlined the current phenomena of goods sufficiency but lack of consumer purchasing power, the lack of capital due to the suspension of external (Russian) aid, and the massive corruption.[32]

Nguyen Van Linh began his report on the first day of the congress by asserting that the Vietnamese people had an "unshakable determination to follow the socialist path under the party leadership," but he added that "the overall profound crisis facing socialist countries has caused socialism to experience an unprecedented fierce criticism from many sides...even in communist ranks."[33] After reiterating the party's commitment to Marxism-Leninism "creatively applied" to Vietnam, Linh acknowledged that past mistakes included overly rapid elimination of the multicomponent economy, establishment of a public ownership system "absolutely occupying superiority over the national economy," and eliminating bureaucratic centralism and state subsidies too slowly. Revised economic principles included advances in line with the development of the production force; building step-by-step production relations from the lower to the higher levels with diversified forms of ownership; developing a multicomponent commodity-based economy, in which the state-run and collective economy will be gradually strengthened; and carrying out various forms of distribution based chiefly on the results of productive labor and economic results. Stripped of its carefully constructed rhetoric, the call remained one of pushing *doi moi* forward in the direction of market-oriented policies and compensation based on productivity despite all obstacles.

Slightly more than one month later, on August 9, Vo Van Kiet succeeded Do Muoi as premier, and some observers saw developments as a triumph for Southern reformers. Kiet brought with him an experienced economist, Phan Van Khai, to serve as deputy prime minister, along with two other Southerners. Closely examined, however, the cabinet, party, and army appear to reflect a continuing fragile balance between diverse factions.[34]

Kiet, once mayor of Ho Chi Minh City, outlined a bold course of action to handle the economic emergency: resort to government bonds rather than the printing presses in an effort to reduce inflation and to induce savings; incentives to stimulate exports; banking reform and other measures to encourage foreign investment, including a reduction in administrative red tape; a continued struggle against corruption, admittedly still omnipresent; and controls over governmental expenditures. The current commitment is to a market-centered economy "as a transitional step toward socialism," but with the transitional period deliberately unspecified.

Although there is a tremendous difference between the attitudes and policies of 1975 and those of 1991 in Vietnam, it remains to be seen whether this society can make the transition from a command to a market-oriented economy with reasonable success and at a cost that is not excruciating. Once again, the commitment to economic reform seems irreversible, whatever oscillations may take place on specific aspects.

Once the successes are tabulated, however, the remaining problems seem very grave. The number of unemployed, as noted, is already staggering. There have been heavy reductions both in military personnel and in governmental employees. Were further reductions to take place along with cuts in governmental subsidies, social problems could easily mount to a dangerous level. Lacking hard currency, the government placed strict controls over foreign exchange earnings at the end of October 1991, so as to be able to finance necessary imports.

Some observers argue that international financial assistance from the World Bank, the International Monetary Fund (IMF), and other sources is essential to the success of the present program, and they therefore urge the United States to lift its embargo, thereby enabling these funds—and others from governments like Japan—to be made available.[35] Others believe that even bolder domestic measures need to be taken, among them a total restructuring of the state sector of the economy to make it market-responsive—an issue, as we have seen, that is also facing China—and the creation of an infrastructure that will give greater encouragement to foreign investment. Whatever the answers—and undoubtedly they involve a combination of measures—Vietnam continues to pay heavily for past policies and for a system that it seems unable either to adjust effectively or to abandon.

Cambodia and Laos

The other two states that together with Vietnam constitute what is called Indochina have gone through their own forms of economic "renovation" in recent years. In Cambodia, the outline of the new economic policies of the Phnom Penh government was presented by Heng Samrin, general secretary of the Kampuchean People's Party, on October 17, 1991, the opening day of an extraordinary party congress called to proclaim a conversion to liberal democracy.[36] Heng asserted that the party and government would implement the principles of a free market economy, recognizing private ownership of land, homes, property, and means of production.

To support agricultural advances, technological improvements would be encouraged, subsidies would be granted, new areas for cultivation would be assisted, and the peasants would have the right to manage their own products freely. In the industrial sector, the state would encourage both local and foreign investment, guaranteeing that there would be no nationalization. Industries using indigenous materials, employing either local or foreign capital, would be favored; and energy, manufacturing, and mineral fields would be made priorities. Special attention would also be given to the improvement of transport and communications. Financial markets, along with banks and insurance agencies, would be liberalized. Clearly, these pledges went as far as any market supporter could desire. The test would lie in their implementation—and in the environment, domestic and international, that would determine Cambodia's future.

Even more than most war-stricken countries, Cambodia has been ravished in recent decades. Economic reform under the People's Revolutionary Party of Cambodia (KPPP) was first promulgated in 1989, with Vietnam's *doi moi* program undoubtedly a stimulus. Yet officials of the Cambodian Ministry of Planning estimated that the 1990 annual per capita income, in constant 1984 dollars, was $170, $10 less than in 1970, 20 years earlier. As much as one-third of the arable land lay idle because of fighting, mines, and displaced individuals. Not surprisingly, agricultural improvement was placed at the top of the agenda in the 1991–1995 economic plan, with funds to import fertilizer and insecticides being sought.

Anxious to draft laws encouraging foreign investors, Phnom Penh officials complained that they lacked the experts for such a task, a commentary on the slaughter and flight of the cream of Cambodia's former intelligentsia. Meanwhile, inflation has continued to rise, with the prices of many food items doubling or tripling from the fall of 1990 to the spring of 1991. The National Bank of Cambodia sought to stabilize the currency by controlling foreign exchange leaving the country. Smuggling and black market activities were rife, and by 1990 Phnom Penh had become a city where illicit wealth was easily visible in the form of Mercedes-Benz automobiles and other conspicuous displays, arousing public resentment and jeopardizing the government's position with the electorate. The gap between Phnom Penh and the countryside also widened.[37] In the final analysis, economics in Cambodia will be dependent upon politics, including the fate of the peace agreement and the projected countrywide elections.

Unlike Cambodia, Laos remained in the Leninist camp and, paralleling Vietnam, sought to turn out economically while holding to the dictatorship of the Laos People's Revolutionary Party. At the Fifth Party Congress opening on March 27, 1991, Kaysone Phomvihan, party general secretary, reported on what he termed "five years of all-round restructuring."[38] He asserted that a "family economy" had been promoted in agriculture and that the government had applied market relations with state sanctions, eliminating "bureaucratic and centralized management mechanisms." Despite the 1987–1988 drought, he claimed that the GNP had increased by nearly 30 percent since 1985 while the population had grown by only 15 percent in the same period. Recent economic growth had averaged 5.5 percent.

Although Laos leans toward Vietnam politically, its economic relations are principally with Thailand. The Mekong River project that would involve these two countries centrally is still in the survey stage, with both political (Vietnamese opposition) and economic difficulties. Meanwhile, some 600 Thai companies are conducting trade with Laos, and such programs as a joint Thai-Lao tourist agency are operating. The Lao government is also looking to China's Yunnan Province for expanded economic relations, suggesting the possibility of another NET. At the same time, the government hopes that capital and technology can be acquired from Thailand and such nations as Japan.

Despite Kaysone's upbeat report, Laos remains very poor and, as recent evidence indicates, strongly dependent upon the weather for adequate food supplies. Local officials reported in December 1991 that Luang Prabang Province faced a rice shortage of more than 122,000 tons because of that year's natural disasters—droughts, floods, and pests.[39] Between 1986 and 1991, the government has received some $962 million in gratis aid and loans, with the funds reportedly used for agriculture, communications, industry, handicrafts, and construction. Foreign investment during the same period amounted to nearly $190 million, most of it committed to small operations.

Whatever their political systems, the Indochina countries
face a major struggle in seeking to come abreast of their
ASEAN neighbors. Years of warfare—not yet fully resolved in
Cambodia and Laos (Hmong resistance continues in some
areas)—relegated economic development to a secondary
position. Mistaken policies compounded the burdens. A brain
drain that has not yet been remedied posed further serious
problems. Moreover, in the highly competitive international
quest for investment, these countries have limited appeal,
except for a few fields such as offshore oil in the case of Vietnam, timber and minerals (raising environmental issues), and
tourism. In each case, however, the old Stalinist developmental model has been abandoned or substantially modified, and a
reform course has been plotted. As indicated, the results will
be dependent upon both domestic and international events.

Mongolia

Even more than Cambodia, Mongolia at this point is an ex-
Leninist state. Its very young leaders have proclaimed their
support not only for market economies but for political pluralism. With breathtaking speed, a group of radical reformers,
mostly in their late twenties and early thirties, have pushed
through a wide range of economic changes. Price controls on
agricultural and consumer goods have ended; new legislation
pertaining to banking, taxes, and selected industries and
designed to support privatization has been enacted; and enterprises previously owned by the state are being auctioned to
private parties.[40]

Unfortunately, the Mongolian economic situation has been
extremely bad. The problem is partly caused by the degree of
past dependence on the Soviet Union. Up to 1990, the USSR
had been providing about $800 million annually in grants and
loans, some $360 per capita for the slightly more than 2
million Mongols whose total per capita income was estimated
variously at from $500 to $900. In May 1990, the Mongolian
deputy premier acknowledged that Mongolia received 40
percent of its consumer goods, 80 percent of its supplies for
the national economy, and 90 percent of its technical machin-

ery from the USSR. Its accumulated debt to Moscow was more than $15 billion.[41]

The worsening of economic conditions in the USSR was reflected in the growing economic crisis in Mongolia. The rapid privatization program, together with price decontrol, produced a serious shock, at least for the short term. By 1991, inflation, severe energy shortages, problems in obtaining necessities like food, rising unemployment, and what officials referred to as "a shadow (second) economy" were manifest. More than 10 percent of the work force was unemployed by mid-1991; emergency shipments of flour were required to offset the inability to harvest wheat caused by gasoline shortages; and a shortage of hard currency made purchases of new equipment impossible. The budget deficit mounted sharply, and the government ordered a curtailment of expenditures by various ministries.

Not surprisingly, a poll taken under the auspices of the Mongolian People's Revolutionary Party (MPRP) in the summer of 1991 indicated that the citizenry, once strong supporters of restructuring, were now critical.[42] Some 70 percent expressed dissatisfaction with the changes taking place in the social, economic, and spiritual life of the country. The swift increase in prices, currency devaluation, unemployment, and the decline in discipline and order were singled out as key problems. Still, Mongolia's current leaders, hopeful of assistance from international agencies like the World Bank and the Asian Development Bank (which Mongolia has joined) and from Japan, the United States, and others, voice their determination to stay with the new program.

No Turning Back

In summary, it is clear that every Asian socialist state, as well as those that are leaving socialism, is now committed to a major economic transformation, and there can be no turning back to the Stalinist model. In the most basic sense, the present course is irreversible, although there will be twists and turns, retreats and advances.

Nonetheless, the evidence also demonstrates conclusively that no easy, painless method of shifting from a command economy to a mixed economy with a strong market orientation has been discovered. Understandably, under these conditions a debate continues to rage about whether it is better to take a gradualist approach to such matters as price decontrol, privatization, and decentralization or to adopt "cold turkey" methods, abandoning the old order quickly and hoping that after the initial shock the economy will respond favorably in time to prevent social disorder.

Certain problems that accompany the socialist economic reforms are especially troubling. Corruption—including corruption of the most pervasive sort—went with Leninism. Privilege for the governing elite and their progeny was built into the political order. Much was hidden from the citizenry, however, and among the public at large, spartanism was more or less shared. Moreover, among the key symbols of Leninist authority, some, including Mao Zedong and Ho Chi Minh, coveted power, not wealth. Now the old forms of corruption linger on, with officialdom and business mixing, low-paid cadres and bureaucrats supplementing their incomes by various illegal transactions, and the children of the elite taking advantage of their positions to become prosperous in the private sector. At the same time, a nouveau riche group is emerging from nonofficial ranks, inciting jealousy. In short, the system, still elitist and based heavily upon contacts, is conducive to massive corruption in a multiplicity of forms. The gap between regions, moreover, combined with the rapid growth of NETs encompassing external areas, raises new political as well as economic issues, especially when coupled with decentralization policies.

Clearly, the state has a role, indeed, a very important role, in any strategy of rapid development. The Japanese model, adapted with modifications by three of the NIEs, namely, South Korea, Taiwan, and Singapore, has a strong appeal in certain socialist and ex-socialist countries of Asia. Nonetheless, the halfway house implicit in efforts such as China's is quite distinct from the manner in which the state was employed in the NIEs, and it is not certain that China and other Leninist states can reach the Japanese model or a reasonable facsimile by following their present course. State ownership, for instance, is not to be confused with state mercantilism. In those states pursuing neomercantilist policies, the government serves as protector of the private sector and in some degree as guide and planner, but it does not own or manage the productive facilities.

It is also difficult to reevaluate the contribution made by different classes to economic and cultural progress and to adjust compensation—both economic and social—accordingly. Priding themselves on being "workers' states," the Leninists have rewarded manual workers, especially those in skilled or arduous categories, relatively better than the wide range one can label intellectuals—scientists, technicians, academics, and professionals. Moreover, in recent times, those in the purely private sector, from taxi drivers and noodle shop operators to peasant marketeers, have emerged high on the economic scale. At the same time, officials have placed a strong premium on upgrading education and emphasizing science and technology. They have praised the intellectuals as indispensable to progress. How is the chasm between words and practice to be bridged?

Further, it is not impossible but it is also not easy to build a work ethic after years of separating productivity and compensation. Similarly, when quantity was the principal criterion of success, namely, meeting assigned quotas, and quality was a secondary consideration, another formidable hurdle to development must be overcome.

Finally, whatever the level of crisis and however much time may be involved, dismantling the command economy is certain to induce many hardships and injustices. The issue of preserving order naturally remains an important consideration, especially in the minds of those who hold power. Thus, the political repercussions of economic reform in Leninist states must be considered, as well as the political route likely to evolve as the remaining socialist states move toward the twenty-first century.

4
Politics in the Late Leninist Era: The Quest for Stability

The People's Republic of China

When Premier Li Peng outlined the Ten-Year Program and the Eighth Five-Year Plan before the National People's Congress on March 25, 1991, he included a brief but all-inclusive statement about the political system to which the Chinese Communist Party was committed.[1] This section opened with the familiar exhortation, "We must unswervingly take the road of building socialism with Chinese characteristics." As noted, the essence of that road was then signaled: make economic development the central task, adhere to the Four Cardinal Principles, and persist in carrying out reform and the outward-looking policy.

The current political creed of the Chinese Leninists is summed up in those four "cardinal principles," and Li proceeded to elaborate upon them. At their heart is the principle of upholding "the people's democratic dictatorship led by the working class and based on the alliance of workers and farmers"—in more straightforward language, maintaining the dictatorship of the Communist Party.

Drawing on the history of earlier Chinese politics and on the belief that a dictatorship can be made more palatable by using united front tactics, Chinese leaders have long espoused what Li called "the system of multiparty cooperation and political consultation under the leadership of the Communist Party" and the consolidation of "the patriotic united front." Since the founding of the People's Republic, the Communists have maintained a number of carefully groomed non-Communist parties, small in size, smaller in power, but useful in portraying representation for nonworker-peasant elements of Chinese society and cultivating the image of a CCP willing to listen to outside advice.

In this portion of his remarks, Li also referred to the need to improve the system of people's congresses and to strengthen the socialist legal system. When Deng and his associates

41

launched their major economic reform program at the end of 1978, political revisions were also put in motion. In the name of socialist legalism, new legal codes were drafted, the judicial system was strengthened, and a pledge was made that henceforth Chinese citizens would not be subject to the arbitrariness of the Mao era. Rather, they would be treated in accordance with the provisions of the law.

In accordance with the Dengist reforms, the authority—or more accurately, the rights—of the National People's Congress were strengthened. Specialized committees of the congress were activated to consider specific types of legislation, and in the congress itself, discussion, sometimes dissent, was permitted. In elections, limited choice was permitted by providing more candidates than seats to be filled, but with all candidates cleared by the CCP. At no time was the legislative branch—either national or provincial—allowed to challenge party and administrative authority.

After touching upon these matters, Li proceeded to mention another cardinal principle, namely, the need to uphold Marxism-Leninism and Mao Zedong Thought as the nation's guiding doctrine. The Chinese Communists, it should be noted, did not reach that specific ideological formulation without difficulty. Like other Asian Leninists, the current CCP leaders of the older generation had undeviatingly sworn allegiance to Leninist-Stalinist doctrines in earlier times, whatever misgivings they may have had about specific Soviet policies from time to time. Trotskyites along with other miscreants were ousted from the party, and Stalin was viewed as the legitimate successor to the Leninist tradition. Correspondingly, Khrushchev was ultimately defined as a revisionist, and no Soviet leader after Stalin was regarded as a significant ideological leader. Chinese nationalism, always latent within the Communist movement, began to rise to the fore in ideological as well as other terms after 1956.

It was thus indispensable that the Chinese Communists find their own ideological spokesman, and who could fit that role more adequately than Mao Zedong? It would have been better, however, if Mao had died in 1957. His erratic policies after that time, culminating in the Great Proletarian Cultural Revolution, discomforted the reformers headed by Deng enormously. Indeed, after 1978, when they returned to power, widespread criticism of Mao was tolerated although Deng himself was always careful to pronounce Mao 70 percent correct and to comment deprecatingly that his own record was not as good.

A formula satisfactory at least to the new leaders was found. Mao Zedong Thought was to be considered the *collective* wisdom of a number of CCP figures, headed by Mao, but with the ideas encompassed in that phrase not exclusively his contribution. It was acknowledged that Mao had made mistakes, some serious, in his later years, but his overall contributions to communism were pronounced outstanding. A pronounced tendency to elevate Mao can be seen in the official propaganda in the more-troubled times since the Tiananmen killings. Thus, in his lengthy speech on the occasion of the 70th anniversary of the Chinese Communist Party on July 1, 1991, Jiang Zemin, party secretary, lauded Mao in reverential terms:

> His theories, lines, policies, and principles concerning the new democratic revolution and socialist revolution, his immortal contributions to the political, economic, cultural, military, and foreign affairs and the building of the party, and his correct thinking on a series of major issues concerning socialist construction have enriched and developed Marxism-Leninism and become our precious ideological wealth.[2]

Jiang made no mention whatsoever of Mao's errors or shortcomings.

In their March and July 1991 speeches, Li and Jiang cited other political principles requiring support. It is revealing that they both paid special attention to the need to develop "relations of equality, mutual assistance, unity, cooperation, and common prosperity" among all of China's nationalities and the importance of opposing "ethnic discrimination and separation of nationalities." China's leaders are well aware of the delicate situation with respect to their non-Han peoples, especially since the disintegration of the Soviet Union and the emergence of independent republics in Central Asia as well as a new Mongolia.

In certain respects, China is still an empire. To be sure, the ethnic minorities are not regime-threatening because they total only 8 percent of the population and, being both diverse and dispersed, cannot unite politically.[3] They occupy vast tracts of China's borderlands, however, and their dissidence can be and indeed has been troubling. The Tibetan case is well known, but there have also been problems with the Uighur in Xinjiang and even with the Mongols in Inner Mongolia. Although the Central Asian peoples are generally in an ethnic-conscious but pre-nationalist stage, should an Islamic nationalism emerge in this region, it might attract China's Islamic peoples or at least a portion of them.

China faces a broader issue of unity, however. This land of more than 1 billion people has long had important subcultural differences of note among the Han, encompassing language, cuisine, and even life-style. The new emphasis on decentralization and the coastal strategy of development, eminently logical from an economic standpoint, raise troublesome political issues. With certain portions of China seeking closer relations with diverse external sources, forming NETs, the centripetal tendencies rise still further.

The Communists have sought to fight the separatism that they inherited from the past by imposing an authoritarian order cemented by single party rule under the tightest, most comprehensive organizational system that nation has ever known. They have also insisted upon strict party control of the military, being well aware of modern China's history of warlordism. Further, a uniform ideological creed has been dispensed continuously in a great variety of ways in an effort to bind all citizens to a single set of beliefs, with a rising nationalist quotient added, thereby supplementing Leninism with an appeal to certain racial-cultural instincts deeply imbedded in the Chinese people.

These techniques were very effective in the opening stages of the regime. Nonetheless, mistaken policies began to take their toll even before the first decade of Communist rule had ended. By the end of the Cultural Revolution, disillusionment among significant sectors of the society, especially the intellectuals but including other elements, even some military personnel, was evident. The reform program commenced in 1979 did much to rebuild confidence, but meanwhile the divisive forces mentioned earlier had begun to operate. Simultaneously, a world was opening before the eyes of the Chinese, especially the better-educated classes. The achievements of the neighboring market economies became known, including those of other Chinese—in Hong Kong, Taiwan, and Singapore.

Meanwhile, the reforms themselves created new volatile issues, notably corruption and privilege, and at the same time made possible more open expressions of dissidence. Those expressions began to spew forth, especially from younger, better-educated urbanites. Bold criticisms were voiced, some of them in widely circulated journals. Under Hu Yaobang and Zhao Ziyang, the arena of freedom widened, although the basic authoritarian structure remained intact.

Then a combination of events occurred: Hu was forced out as party general secretary; the overheated economy resulted in mounting inflation; the Communist Party was rent with serious cleavages about what remedial actions to take; and the reverberations of the political earthquake shaking the Western socialist states began to reach China. With these developments and with a host of previous grievances unanswered, the stage was set for the events that took place in the spring of 1989.

The Tiananmen "counterrevolution," as the conservatives in the top Communist hierarchy termed it, both frightened and angered the supreme elite, including Deng Xiaoping.[4] The subsequent measures attempted might be defined as "punishment and reform." Those involved in the Tiananmen incident who were regarded as guilty of sedition or committing other crimes were brought before courts, tried privately, and given diverse sentences, depending in part on whether they repented. Those who insisted that they were innocent were often given heavy punishment. Wang Juntao, a newspaper editor, for example, received a 13-year sentence, as did the economist Chen Ziming. It should be remembered, moreover, that some dissidents of an earlier era remain in prison, among them Wei Jingsheng, whose bold denunciation of communism as another form of totalitarianism akin to fascism earned him a 15-year sentence in the fall of 1979. If any of those accused of counterrevolutionary acts were found innocent, that fact has not been revealed.

The death sentence was reserved for individuals convicted of the destruction of property or lives, and so far as can be determined, no students were executed. (It is ironic that certain classic Chinese principles still apply under the "proletarian dictatorship": one punishes students but does not execute them—that supreme sanction is reserved for commoners.) A large number of students were imprisoned, however, and although many, declared repentant, have been released, an undisclosed number remain in detention.

Meanwhile, political "reform" got under way and is continuing. An effort is being made to reshape young intellectuals by restoring the political methods of the 1950s—extensive indoctrination using the collected works of Mao, Deng, and others. Past heroes are also being resurrected, including Li Feng, the feckless young military man who served his comrades and community selflessly. As noted, Mao Zedong is at present being described in highly laudatory terms.

The freedom to criticize has been greatly circumscribed unless the criticism is of the type already voiced by official sources. With tens of thousands of students overseas and unwilling to return, permission to study abroad, especially in the United States, has also been curtailed. Party and security surveillance of China's institutions of higher learning has been increased, particularly at times when unauthorized political demonstrations are feared.

Although homage is paid to Marxism-Leninism in China's new ideological campaign and a new edition of Lenin's collected works in Chinese has recently been published, the central appeal to the Chinese people, as was indicated earlier, is increasingly based on nationalism. Jiang's anniversary speech is a striking example. He began with a depiction of modern Chinese history that credited the Communists with having led the final campaign to liberate China from imperialism and feudalism. "The Chinese people have stood up!" Jiang proclaimed. But a new risk looms on the horizon, according to Jiang and others: using "peaceful evolution" as their weapon, foreign forces are seeking to undermine Chinese socialism and reimpose external imperialist control over China.[5]

Communist spokesmen claim that the concept of "peaceful evolution" was first advanced by John Foster Dulles as a means of subverting the People's Republic. Nevertheless, the phrase seems an unfortunate choice for the CCP because the alternatives would appear to be violent upheaval or stagnation. Once adopted as a central target, however, it cannot be abandoned. And although the finger is pointed primarily at the United States and the powerful role of the U.S. media at the time of Tiananmen, in reality, as the Chinese leaders know, the external influences operating upon the Chinese people come ever more strongly from China's dynamic Asian neighbors.

In any case, the challenge to Leninism from political pluralism is equated with interference in China's internal affairs, thereby linking the defense of socialism with the defense of China's national integrity. Over-Westernization, it is asserted, destroys the dignity of the Chinese people and the cultural heritage of this great nation—words almost identical to those uttered by China's Confucian savants more than a century ago.

When one probes the core of the present leadership's concern, however, the issue is domestic stability. Political pluralism, as Jiang frankly acknowledged, would undermine the leadership of the Communist Party and split the nation. China's chosen route is different: "The people's democratic dictatorship," asserted Jiang, "combines the exercise of democracy among the people with dictatorship over the enemies of the people." (The party naturally defines who are people and who are enemies.) The Western multiparty system is both unwise and unnecessary: "The system of multiparty cooperation and political consultation under the leadership of the Chinese Communist Party" provides the appropriate political means to unite the entire people around the goal of "socialist modernization." Also, "the democratic parties are participants in state affairs; they are not out of office, nor are they opposition parties." Jiang's central theme is clear: Is this not a system superior to the rule of capitalists, epitomized by "bourgeois liberalization," and the cacophony of discordant voices heard under that system?[6]

Still, current Chinese Communist leaders, whether "conservative" or "progressive," cannot avoid awareness of the CCP's damaged reputation at present. Thus, while they laud the party's great accomplishments, past and present, and refer to its membership of some 50 million as reflecting public trust, they also exhort members to tackle the party's inner problems. Once again, blame is generously assigned to outsiders. "As China carries out reform, opens to the outside world, and develops a commodity economy," said Jiang in his July speech,

> decadent capitalist ideas, values, and ways of life will unavoidably take advantage of our weak points to break in and contaminate the body of our party. Peaceful evolution and bourgeois liberalization pose a practical threat to our country's independence and sovereignty and to our development, reform, and opening up. Under these circumstances, some of our party organizations have indeed become weak and lax in their discipline. Some of our party members and cadres failed to withstand certain tests, became muddle-headed and showed a lack of firm political stand. Others even violated the law or standards of discipline and became degenerate. Still others have obdurately clung to bourgeois liberalization and discarded national and personal dignity, standing in opposition to the party and the people.[7]

The first answer to these problems, continued Jiang, was for all party members to improve their ideological understanding. Second, members had to be aware of the need to serve the people, keeping close ties with the masses. (The exhortation "Listen to the voice of the people" has deep roots in Chinese tradition, and it continues to be the cry—as it was among the students in Tiananmen square, whose appeal, at least initially, was not for parliamentary democracy but for the leaders to hold a dialogue with them and listen to their grievances.) Jiang acknowledged that some party members served themselves rather than their flock and that those guilty of greed and corruption should be severely punished. He refrained from indicating how widespread these practices were.

Third, it was important to strengthen party organization and to eliminate factionalism at all costs. That included tightening organizational structure in the rural areas and carrying the ideological message to the peasants who still constituted some three-fourths of China's population and who had little knowledge of, or concern about, MLM (Marxism-Leninism-Mao

Thought). Finally, looking to the future, Jiang asserted that successors to the older generation must be sought and trained: they should be young, well educated, and attuned to the tasks of socialist modernization.[8]

Neither of the speeches by Li and Jiang made direct reference to external criticisms of China's human rights record, but at the beginning of November 1991 a lengthy White Paper on Human Rights in China was issued.[9] Although it could be convincing only to those already convinced, it is interesting for several reasons.

In defense of China's human rights policies, the White Paper intertwines national and human rights, devoting extensive attention to the struggle of China against imperialism and the painful process of establishing national sovereignty: The founding of the PRC "put an end to the nation's history of dismemberment, oppression, and humiliation at the hands of alien powers" as well as to the "long years of turbulence characterized by incessant war and social disunity." A militant nationalism permeates the document.

At the same time, there is a complete denial that any rights of individuals are violated. The Chinese people are "masters of their country." They elect their representatives, and the National People's Congress is "the supreme organ of state power." The CCP is "the ruling party of socialist China," but "its leadership position has been the result of the historical choice made by the Chinese people." Moreover, "it conducts its activities within the framework of the Constitution and the law." The multiparty cooperation whereby the eight democratic parties work with the CCP for the general welfare of the people, together with the Chinese People's Political Consultative Conference (CPPCC), which consists of representatives of all political parties and social organizations, provides for a system of political consultation that promotes democracy. "China's human rights legislation and policies are endorsed and supported by the people of all nationalities and social strata and by all the political parties, social organizations, and all walks of life." How can critics be so shortsighted!

In addition, however, the White Paper raises issues long present in the debate between Leninists and liberal democrats about human rights. The foremost human right for the Chinese people is proclaimed to be the right to subsistence—food, clothing, and shelter—and these rights have been achieved, thanks to the CCP.

As noted, the White Paper will convince very few liberals. What is truly important about this document, however, is that it signifies that the present PRC leaders take seriously China's international reputation. Despite their repeated charge that such external criticism represents unwarranted interference in their nation's internal affairs, they finally felt it necessary to respond to the barrage of criticism that followed the Tiananmen incident (and, indeed, preceded it as well). The next step is to involve the PRC in a multilateral discussion of all aspects of the issue in a manner akin to the conference that resulted in the Helsinki accords.

Considerable attention has been paid to the recent major speeches of two frontline Chinese leaders and to the White Paper because by reading them carefully, one can discern much about the current state of Chinese politics. What are its essential features? First, a generational change is at hand, and all Chinese see this as a transitional period. In a very few years, the octogenarians who hold supreme power (albeit often without portfolios) will be gone.[10] Chinese politics is sufficiently personalized—and delicately balanced—that the order of their death may be important. In any case, there is considerable doubt as to whether the men currently operating under their supervision, including Li Peng and Jiang Zemin, can retain their posts after their mentors are gone.

Will there be a reversal of the verdict on Tiananmen, as there was on the activities of student protesters in the same spot at the time of Zhou Enlai's death in 1976? Will such a reversal bring about the rehabilitation of Zhao Ziyang, who remains in limbo but unpunished (perhaps because of Deng's reported protection), or, more likely, will it elevate the power of those labeled "progressives," some of whom operate at higher governmental levels, including a few who were Zhao's associates?

One supremely important fact warrants attention. The remnants of the first-generation revolutionaries who are still at the helm in China, whatever their recent activities, are generalists. They have had a lengthy history of involvement—and all-important personal connections—in every facet of Chinese governance. Hence, they have a reach into party, government, and the military that those who follow will perforce be incapable of achieving. Thus, collective leadership will become increasingly essential. But can China operate smoothly under such leadership? In this century, a *primus inter pares* always emerged: Yuan Shih-kai, Chiang Kai-shek, Mao Zedong, Deng Xiaoping. Otherwise, political disorder prevailed. Has the situation changed?

Decentralization, so essential from an economic standpoint, seems irreversible whatever periodic retrenchments take place. How will this affect the politics of the center? To date, promising—or threatening—individuals like Li Ruihuan of Tianjin, Zhu Rongji of Shanghai, and Ye Xuanping of Guangdong have been coopted by the center. Apart from individual figures of prominence, however, the provincial and metropolitan governments are exercising greater independence, as is demonstrated by spreading diversities in policy. Where will the balance be struck?

Meanwhile, figures like Yang Baibang, the half-brother of President Yang Shangkun, who serves as secretary of the Central Military Commission and director of the People's Liberation Army General Political Department, are putting great stress on intensive political training for China's armed forces and the critical importance of party control over the military. (Some commanders, backed by a number of senior retirees, including Long March veterans, resisted using troops against civilians at the time of the Tiananmen killings.) In the military as well as the party, a great generational transition is under way, and younger officers are interested in the modernization of equipment; they watched the Gulf War on television. The classic Maoist doctrine of men over weapons is passé, but there is validity in Mao's other dictum: power comes out of the barrel of a gun. The old men at the helm today have not forgotten that fact.[11]

In sum, although there has been a perceptible tightening of restraints on political openness by Beijing authorities, giving the appearance of a tough regime hunkering down politically and in full control, in reality the central PRC government is weaker at present than it has been at any time since the

Cultural Revolution. This is illustrated by its uncertain reach to the provinces and, notably, the South; its limited capacity to induce loyalty; and the "second" (private) politics, as well as the second economy, that now exists on a widening scale.

To the extent their mood can be measured—and there are no public opinion polls available—a strong majority of the Chinese people are largely unresponsive to the current political exhortation. The attitude, at least among most younger, educated individuals, is a mixture of cynicism and indifference toward politics. Ideological faith is in very limited supply. Among all elements of the population, the thrust is toward improving one's livelihood. When the leaders talk in worried tones about the rise of materialism, hedonism, and selfishness—every person for himself or herself—they are exposing a growing tendency.[12]

Present leaders realize very well that the fate of the party and their regime will rest upon the ability of the government, central and local, to satisfy the rising expectations of the citizenry. For this reason alone, economic policies must take priority, and there can be no turning back from the program defined as one of "reform and turning out." The key dilemma is how to preserve political stability in the midst of socioeconomic changes at home and a sweeping revolution abroad, with socialism under multiple challenges and what the true believers call "contamination" an omnipresent threat.

China's basic course was strongly reaffirmed in mid-March 1992 at a meeting of the 20-member Politburo, where it was determined that economic construction remained the central task and that while vigilance should be maintained against "right deviation," principal attention should be devoted to guarding against "left deviation." These words signal a strong commitment to the economic reforms initiated by Deng. At the same time, opposition to political pluralism remains unwavering. Thus, the effort to pursue a dual course, whatever its inner contradictions, has been reemphasized.

The Democratic People's Republic of Korea

The Democratic People's Republic of Korea has not reached this stage, yet there is growing evidence that a similar concern exists among the top elite that such risks lie ahead. In most respects, North Korea is a traditional, not a revolutionary, society. Here the cult of personality, borrowing heavily from ancient rites relating to shamanism, has reached an unprecedented intensity, surpassing the adoration of Stalin or Mao at its height: Kim Il Sung is omniscient and omnipresent. Here also, xenophobia has been cultivated and preserved, with the common people more isolated than in any other Leninist society—although cracks are beginning to appear. Here, life is very simple: hard, monotonous work, a spartan livelihood centering upon the household, and very limited mobility.

There is one respect, however, in which North Korea is modern. Its leaders have learned the technique of mass mobilization. Whether participating in the orchestrated demonstrations on special occasions or gathered for party rallies or listening to the Great Leader over radio or television, the populace is subjected to an intensive political barrage, an effort to ensure absolute loyalty and complete solidarity.

The formal DPRK political structure is classic Leninism with some of the same modifications adopted in China. In theory, the party and the government have been separated, the former having the function of laying down the broad policy lines, the latter charged with policy implementation. In fact, however, the leading political figures hold a multiplicity of positions that render such distinctions dubious and party dominance unchallengeable.

Quite possibly, North Korea has achieved the most intensive organizational network of any Leninist state. In addition to the Korean Workers' Party (Communist), or KWP, which at one point claimed that its members constituted 14 percent of the adult population, there are pre-party organizations in the form of the League of Socialist Working Youth and the Young Pioneers that encompass most young people. Apart from these, there are a large variety of popular front bodies, with separate industrial laborer, farmer, women, student, professional, Christian, and Buddhist associations.[13]

The Great Leader, Kim Il Sung, holds the office of president, and a cabinet system is in effect, headed by a premier. Like the other Asian Leninist states, North Korea has a nominal multiparty system, with the Korean Social Democratic

Party and the Chondoguo Chongu (Heavenly way young friends) Party operating "under the leadership of the KWP." Moreover, a Supreme People's Assembly exists, with various committees within it to consider legislation. At the province, county, and city levels, there are People's Assemblies. On November 24, 1991, the North Korean Central Broadcasting Station reported that a total of 26,074 unopposed candidates for city and county assemblies had been elected, with 99.89 percent of the eligible voters going to the polls and all candidates receiving 100 percent support.[14] Under the DPRK system, voters do not choose among alternative candidates, but cast a yes or no vote for the Korean Workers' Party nominees.

What is important with respect to DPRK politics is not the formal structure, but the manner in which Leninism operates in this great citadel of Stalinist conservatism. The order of listing in the KWP Politburo provides the first vital information. At the top is the 80-year-old Kim Il Sung, the leader with the longest tenure in the world. The cult surrounding Kim, assiduously cultivated for decades, is unequaled. At the same time, evidence accumulates that governmental operations are now in the hands of his son and the heir apparent, Kim Jung Il. It is likely that the elder Kim's imprimatur is required for all truly important measures but, like Deng Xiaoping, he appears to have assumed a position behind the black curtain, as his age and Asian tradition dictate. Recent reports are that even foreign policy is being shifted to the young Kim, and it has been officially announced that he has become supreme commander of North Korea's military forces.

Although elaborate preparations for the succession have been made, including a growing number of eulogistic accounts of his accomplishments and abilities and the publication of major works under his name, Kim Jung Il remains a mystery, at least to individuals outside the upper layer of DPRK officialdom.[15] He has rarely conducted substantive conversations with foreign visitors, even those from socialist states. Rumors circulate that his tastes run in the direction of fast cars and attractive women, but only his avidity for motion pictures, including foreign films, has been firmly established. Reports regarding his work habits, political inclinations, and abilities vary widely.

Amidst many uncertainties, several facts are clear. Young Kim has surrounded himself with a number of individuals of his approximate age (close to 50), thus bringing to the fore the next generation of top officials. This generation is better educated and more technocratically inclined than the old Kapsan guerrilla group that rose under Kim Il Sung's banner. The changes now under way in DPRK economic policy as well as those in the foreign policy realm may stem from necessity, but they are taking place under the supervision of the successor generation.

It is also certain that after his father's death, Kim Jung Il will have to depend upon performance rather than charisma for his legitimacy and that of his government. Despite the enormous efforts that are going into the portrayal of the young Kim as a truly superior individual, there cannot be two messiahs.

One other individual high in the North Korean political firmament should be mentioned, namely, O Jin-u, senior general, third-ranking member of the Politburo (after the Kims, father and son) and vice chairman of the National Defense Commission (also after the two Kims). O, always seen in the company of one or both of the Kims, is one of the remaining military veterans, comrade-in-arms of Kim Il Sung and a symbol of the importance of military-civilian unity and the role of the military in guarding the throne.

Although there are as yet no signs of significant change in DPRK domestic politics, sooner or later the economic changes already en route will trigger political alterations, protestations notwithstanding.[16] There are several groups within the society to watch, elements that are likely to be in the forefront of supporting, perhaps initiating, changes. First, there are thousands of North Koreans, mostly young, who have had an educational experience abroad—in Eastern Europe, the USSR, or China. However confined their activities, they have seen and heard something of the outer world and its diversities. Second, there are more than 100,000 Koreans now living in the North who once lived in Japan and who began coming back after a Japan-DPRK repatriation agreement in 1959. Reports indicate that many suffer discrimination, but some—particularly those with access to funds from Japan—are playing a role in the society and under certain circumstances might contribute more. There is also a sizable number of military men and diplomats who have had assignments overseas, including in the West. Indeed, the upper political elite, whether at home or abroad, has access to information denied the ordinary citizen. They are not ignorant of the revolution sweeping the world and the dynamic progress of the market economies.

As noted earlier, even the average North Korean citizen, at least those living in the major cities, has increasing access to knowledge about the external environment through visiting relatives from abroad, tourists from various countries, and resident foreign technicians, mostly from the USSR and Eastern Europe, who have been working in the DPRK. If contacts with the South proliferate, a powerful new force with profound political implications will have been introduced, a fact of which every North Korean official is aware.

To date, however, the North Korean government has relied heavily upon three interrelated messages in soliciting support from its people. The first is fear: the U.S. imperialists and the South Korean militarist, fascist regime are poised to attack and destroy the DPRK. The second is that safety lies only in iron-clad unity under leader-party-nation, a trinity that cannot be separated. The third is that only by unremitting labor, with one individual accomplishing the tasks of ten, can the nation be protected from external predators and the glories of socialism be fully achieved.[17]

Even more than China and Vietnam, North Korea now resorts to nationalism rather than Marxism-Leninism to defend its system. The all-encompassing symbol is *chuch'e*. No word is more frequently invoked, and around it an elaborate philosophy has been woven. According to Kim Jung Il, the idea was founded by his father many years earlier, thus providing "our age, the age of independence, with a new guiding ideology."[18] Young Kim continues: "The Juche [*chuch'e*] idea is a man-centered outlook on the world. It has clarified the essential qualities of man as a social being with independence, creativity, and consciousness. It has, on this basis, evolved the new philosophical principle that man is the master of everything and decides everything."[19] If this principle does not seem either new or profound to the outsider, perhaps the nonbeliever does not have the ability to probe the subtleties of *chuch'e*.

In Kim's 1991 tract, *Our Socialism Centered on the Masses Shall Not Perish,* just cited, Marxism-Leninism is never mentioned. The Great Leader is given credit for creating an entirely new ideology, advancing original theories and systematizing them, even though many themes here and in North Korean literature elsewhere parallel Chinese political themes. It is admitted, for example, that these are difficult times for the global socialist movement; and often a defiant tone is adopted, to the effect that even if we have to stand alone, we will preserve socialism because it is the desire of our people.

Bourgeois democracy is described as fraudulent, and "the imperialists and reactionaries" who are posing as champions of human rights, vilifying socialism, are the true terrorists against innocent people.[20] When dealing with opponents, the level of violence in DPRK propagandistic language is striking. Some observers ascribe it to culture, others to the defensiveness of a small state surrounded by bigger and generally more powerful neighbors. In any case, the danger of outsiders subverting Korean socialism is portrayed in much the same manner as it is in Beijing: "The slightest slackening of ideological education," asserts Kim, "may result in the wind of bourgeois liberalism blowing in. It is a stereotyped trick of imperialists to try to smuggle their ideas into other countries, prior to undisguised aggression."

Three fascinating questions remain for the foreign observer seeking to understand the underlying essence of current North Korean politics. First, do the DPRK citizens *believe*? Are they loyal to the Great Leader and to the Dear Leader? Do they believe what they are told—about themselves, about their society, and about the world? Are they prepared to die if necessary to defend socialism? No definitive answers can be given to these questions, although parallels with Nazi Germany and wartime Japan come to mind. There is no hard evidence to contradict the thesis that the overwhelming majority of North Koreans are loyal to the current leadership and system, although anecdotes telling of sporadic dissidence are heard, some of them from Russians who have had greater familiarity with the scene than others. At the same time, logic dictates that in the process of opening North Korea to the world, a series of shocks to the citizenry is likely—and perhaps some gnawing doubts have already begun to make themselves felt.

Closely related to those questions is the question whether the recent propaganda lines can be retained if present trends continue. For example, if the North and South consummate the promising agreement on mutual nuclear inspection that was reached as 1991 ended and if the United States progresses with troop and military exercise reductions as well as upgrading its contacts with the DPRK, how will the "fear" theme be affected? If greater access to the South takes place along with improvements in relations with Japan and the United States, will "ironclad unity" hold? If technological innovations are introduced and a deeper sense of how labor operates elsewhere is gained, will Stakhanovite appeals still carry weight?

Finally, there is the highly personal matter of Kim Il Sung's relationship to the system. When Kim passes from the scene, what will be the political result? Some observers believe that once the Great Leader is gone, neither Kim Jung Il nor any other individual or group can successfully manage the transition that the DPRK must undergo. On the other hand, it may be equally or more plausible to assume that with or without young Kim, a military-technocratic elite can preserve a reasonably high level of political authoritarianism while speeding up economic modernization. The Park Chong Hee era in the South offers one example, despite great differences between the South when the Park period began and the North when the post-Kim Il Sung period will start.

One matter seems certain. Even in this remarkably stable, extremely conservative society, the status quo cannot be maintained for long. The forces of change—economic, scientific-technological, generational—are at the door. The questions relate to when and how these forces will alter this monument to an earlier political age.

Vietnam

Vietnam's Communist leaders remain determined to combine economic reform and a political monopoly of power. At the opening session of the Seventh Party Congress on June 24, 1991, the veteran CPV general secretary, Nguyen Van Linh, delivered a political report whose main theme was that the Vietnamese people had resolved not to accept any path other than the socialist one. A proletarian dictatorship would be maintained involving a worker-peasant-intellectual alliance under the leadership of the Communist Party.

As in the past, Linh vigorously rejected political pluralism in the form of a multiparty system and asserted, "We should be vigilant against demagogic maneuvers which take advantage of the democratic banner to stir up disturbances."[21] Some people, he continued, argued that only with the existence of opposition parties and factions can there be democracy, but that was false: in the former "Saigon puppet government" there were many parties, but no democracy. Given the situation in which Vietnam found itself, he continued, there was no need to establish an opposition. "To accept the multiparty system of opposition is to create conditions for the reactionary forces of revenge within the country and from abroad to rear their heads immediately and legally to operate against the homeland, the people, and the regime. Our people definitely reject this."[22]

It is not clear how many citizens Linh had consulted. His speech and the ambience that surrounded the Seventh Party Congress, however, reveal much about the state of contemporary Vietnamese politics. To an extraordinary extent, Linh and others speaking at the congress acknowledged that public disillusionment with the Vietnam Communist Party and politics in general was extensive; that many party branches were in partial or total decay; that corruption and privilege had separated cadres from the people in a very large number of cases; and that these problems needed urgent attention.

One excerpt from his report indicates an awareness of the situation if not a willingness to undertake drastic structural changes:

The problem remains as to what we should do to secure adequate democracy under one-party leadership. We must scrupulously reflect on this issue with an adequate sense of responsibility to the people. Well aware of this, our party has sought to renovate itself and seek various mechanisms, forms, and specific and effective procedures to allow for accomplishing adequate democracy within the party and in social life.[23]

More than its Leninist neighbors, the Hanoi government has permitted criticisms of political as well as economic policies. A remarkable interview with Bui Tin, the former deputy editor of the party organ, *Nhan Dan,* in Paris in early 1991 was published in a Vietnamese journal, *Que Me,* in that city.[24] Tin, in France for medical treatment, insisted that he intended to return to Vietnam; and in certain respects he defended the current system, indicating that the right to criticize had been greatly expanded. One of his more poignant statements laments the fact that he was criticized by overseas refugees: "What they (the critics) don't realize is that in Vietnam, the outstanding people are all in the Communist Party. . . . If I separate myself from the party, I will become an exile."[25]

Tin also indicated that preparations should be undertaken to move toward political pluralism, asserting "we must calmly expand democracy." He acknowledged that a crisis of confidence existed, with widespread public displeasure. He expressed sympathy with dissidents like Duong Thu Huong, Ta Ba Ton, and Nguyen Ho, individuals reportedly under surveillance, while asserting that he did not necessarily agree with all of their views.[26]

Bui Tin's future remains uncertain; he has been expelled from the party. Moreover, an illustration of the limits on political criticism, even in the case of highly placed figures, is provided by Tran Xuan Bach. Bach, who ranked ninth in the Politburo and was once regarded as a leading figure in ideological matters, was removed from his post in March 1990 after calling for greater democracy and insisting that Vietnam could not walk with one long leg (economic reform) while the other leg was short (political reform).[27]

In his report, Linh took note that thousands of suggestions regarding changes in the party draft document had come at the party's request, and that some had consisted of either "vastly different opinions" warranting study or, in "rare cases," viewpoints "alien to our party and people." Some vigorous debates had previously taken place in the Vietnamese National Assembly despite its controlled character. Moreover, remarkably forthright criticisms of the party and cadre conduct have been published in the press. The general political atmosphere resembles that in China in the mid-1980s prior to the post-Tiananmen crackdown.

The Seventh Party Congress approved limited political liberalization. In the 1992 National Assembly elections, every citizen will have the right to run, not just those approved by the party as in the past. Presumably, multiple candidacies will be allowed, although not under party labels other than the Vietnam Communist Party.

Possibly of greater significance are the revisions of the 1980 constitution officially drafted by a special commission of the National Assembly and scheduled to be promulgated soon. Those extensive revisions augment the power of the government, in the process emphasizing the rule of law (rather than party fiat). Theoretically, the separation of powers between the party and state has been made more explicit, with the cabinet responsible for policy execution and the National Assembly having a genuine law-making role.

Much will depend upon how these new provisions are interpreted and implemented. Similar legal changes were made in China in the course of Deng's initial reforms, and even earlier in North Korea. Fundamentally, they did not alter the monopolistic power of the Communist Party. In Vietnam also, there is not likely to be any immediate deviation from party dominance. Its 2 million members out of a population of 67.5 million will continue to speak for the nation politically, via the traditional "democratic centralism" that reposes genuine power in the hands of the very few.

In Vietnam, there are currently not even the tame "democratic parties" existing in China and North Korea. They have been allowed to disappear quietly. There is, however, a wide range of mass organizations, some of which may have a greater potential for championing political change than artificial parties would have had.

The Seventh Party Congress also put its seal on the process of generational change—lightly. The 76-year-old Linh was replaced as party secretary by the 74-year-old Do Muoi, and shifts in the 13-man Politburo reduced the average age from 71

to near 60. Moreover, there are various signs that with generational change, a dissolution of the old factional alignments is
under way. As in the other Asian Leninist states, a transitional
era is gradually beginning, with the first-generation revolutionaries leaving the active stage.[28]

As noted earlier, the 69-year-old Vo Van Kiet, who assumed the premiership on August 9, 1991, is regarded as an
economic reformer, and with him have come additional Southerners. Those Western scholars and journalists who argued
during the Vietnam War that the National Liberation Front of
South Vietnam (NLFSV) should be distinguished from the
Northern Communists, and in victory would maintain a more
broadly gauged coalition with progressive non-Communists,
were 90 percent wrong. Those NLFSV leaders who refused to
march to Hanoi's tune quickly faded away. Some were "reedu-
cated" or fled. It is true, however, that a North-South cleavage
continues to exist, exacerbated by the different economic
inheritances—and current conditions—in the two regions. The
South, moreover, seems to furnish a majority of the Communist reformers—and also the greater number of strong dissidents both inside and outside the party.

As in other Asian Leninist societies, the current and future
role of the military is a matter of paramount importance—and
one upon which prediction is hazardous.[29] The key military
figures have almost always been closely integrated with the
party, holding high posts in the Politburo and Central Committee. The current defense minister, Le Duc Anh, ranks second
in the Politburo, ahead of the new premier. In general, as
might be expected, the military—and the very sizable security
apparatus existing beside it—is regarded as conservative,
fearful of disorder, and suffering withdrawal symptoms as a
result of the decision to leave Cambodia and the major force
reductions that have taken place in the last two years.

Are the key military figures unified politically, and are the
generational differences significant here, as seems likely in
China and North Korea? The leading Vietnamese military
figures, unlike their counterparts in the other two Asian
Leninist states, have been engaged in almost continuous
warfare for 40 years—against the French, Americans, their

Southern brethren, Cambodian opponents, and Chinese. Their demands on the society have been extraordinarily heavy in terms of lives lost, military expenditures, and development opportunities postponed. Almost certainly the civilianization process now under way for many soldiers is a painful one, particularly with an unemployment rate of close to 20 percent and, hence, limited opportunities for new employment. It would be amazing if military leaders were happy with current trends. Will they be content to allow technocrats to try to improve economic matters and possibly initiate further political changes?

In assessing the Vietnamese political scene, the operative term is "delicate." Faced with desperate economic conditions, the leadership determined first in 1986, and more firmly in 1989, to begin a process of economic reform. Although the results have been decidedly mixed, the economic alterations have progressed to a point where they could only be reversed by some massive political upheaval, a most unlikely development. Meanwhile, Leninism was toppled throughout the West; and in Vietnam, even within the Vietnam Communist Party, the demands for political reform grew louder. Economic crisis fed political discontent; and with the party riddled with corruption at every level, respect for it dwindled to a low ebb.

Under these circumstances, it is not surprising that party veterans rejected political pluralism as a formula for disunity. As in other Asian Leninist states, one refrain is constantly heard: the danger of *bat an* (instability). Yet the voices of discontent were so numerous and powerful that safety valves had to be allowed. Thus, remarkable attacks upon the prevailing politics—even the political system—were made through various channels. At some points, party officials felt compelled to crack down on critics, but the cutoff point shifted and seemed to have no fixed line. Hundreds, perhaps thousands, of individuals defined as enemies of the state or holding views alien to socialism were incarcerated or placed under regular surveillance; but the public mood of political cynicism, especially in the South, surpassed that in China. For the leaders, and the Vietnam Communist Party, this is a precarious time.[30]

Cambodia, Laos, and Mongolia

On October 17, 1991, the Pracheachon Party or Cambodian People's Party (CPP), formerly known as the People's Revolutionary Party of Cambodia, held an extraordinary party congress in Phnom Penh. At this congress, the abandonment of Marxism-Leninism was approved, and the hammer and sickle were removed from the CPP emblem. Heng Samrin, general secretary, reading the new CPP political platform, announced that the party "will organize the state democratically, with legislative, executive, and judicial powers. The president and assembly will be elected through universal, direct, and secret ballot. The government will be responsible to the assembly."[31] Further, "the political structure is that of a liberal democracy and is multiparty," with full political competition allowed.[32]

The same document, as was noted earlier, made a commitment to a free market economy, going far beyond the economic pledges of Vietnam or Laos. These changes had been approved by a 48-member Central Committee, and they were ratified at the October congress by several hundred delegates.

The Cambodian future is sufficiently uncertain to warrant extreme caution. Despite an operating coalition government in the capital under Prince Sihanouk and a respite from civil war, it is by no means clear whether these conditions will hold and whether Cambodia can move into a era of internal peace and openness, political as well as economic. The Khmer Rouge have had a substantial military force, and beyond this, significant grass-roots organizing ability. Some observers believe that by playing upon the weaknesses of the CPP and of the Sihanouk-Son Sann forces as well, the KR can do well in elections, especially in those rural areas where it has control or influence. There is no evidence, moreover, that the KR has abandoned Leninism as have the erstwhile Communists of Phnom Penh.

The extraordinary volte-face of the CPP leaders must also be carefully monitored. The CPP, initially sponsored by Vietnam, has had a history of internal dissent at every level. The key figures, it will be recalled, were all once Khmer Rouge cadres who broke with the Pol Pot faction in the late 1970s, not over policies that came later to be defined as genocidal but over internal struggles and issues of foreign allegiance. Since the October conference, Heng Samrin has stepped aside, and the key CPP figures are the youthful, intense premier, Hun Sen, and Chea Sim, chairman of the party. The CPP leaders have worked hard to create an alliance with Sihanouk's party, but that has been derailed, at least for the present. Sihanouk himself heads the Supreme National Council, the coalition government harboring all four factions; and despite the assault by a Cambodian mob upon the KR leader, Khieu Samphan, shortly after his arrival in Phnom Penh on November 30, the Khmer Rouge decided to continue to work within the coalition.

It is obvious that the major changes made by the CPP were the product of necessity, not ideological conversion. If Sihanouk's cooperation were to be obtained, and the broad program first sketched by the five permanent members of the United Nations Security Council and subsequently approved by the four Khmer factions were to have any chance of becoming operative, the rules that had governed the Phnom Penh government and party had to be changed. Now Cambodia awaits national elections. All groups except the Khmer Rouge are counting heavily on Prince Sihanouk to win the support of a majority of the populace and, despite his mercurial qualities, serve as a stabilizing political force.[33]

Meanwhile, Laos continues along the Leninist political path, strongly in the shadow of Vietnam—but enjoying an increasingly warm economic embrace from Thailand—and Mongolia continues to attempt to make democracy work amid multiple economic problems.[34]

The Old Politics vs. The New Economics

In surveying the Asian Leninist political landscape, three broad conclusions are warranted. First, the remaining Leninist leaders have been pushed onto the defensive. A combination of global developments—most particularly, the collapse of communism in Eastern Europe and the old USSR, and serious economic problems at home—has created an atmosphere of apprehension. To be sure, a torrent of brave words is forthcoming from the leadership, including the timeworn Leninist thesis that socialism is the wave of the future, and whatever the twists and turns, ultimate victory will be achieved; but talk of "very difficult circumstances" and "dangerous shoals surrounding us" reveals the depth of concern.

Second, the responses are varied, but one trend is uniform: nationalism has become the great weapon in the defense of Leninism. The Asian Communists have always had a strong nationalist quotient, but never has it been so extensively—on occasion, exclusively—displayed as at present. The extreme example is to be found in North Korea, where Marxism-Leninism is almost never mentioned. In China and Vietnam also, however, the oft-repeated thesis is that dangerous foreign forces, having failed to subdue the new nation militarily, are now resorting to "peaceful evolution" in an effort to undermine faith in socialism and destroy the dignity of the nation, placing the country under the imperialist yoke of the past.

Alongside the angry blasts at foreign interference in another's internal affairs, however, there is a continuing effort to seize and hold the word "democracy" for the Leninist system. This takes various forms. Bourgeois liberalism is denounced as plutocracy, not government for, by, and of the people. The pledge to listen to the people's voice is regularly made, in accordance with Asian tradition; and in some instances, this includes consulting "democratic parties" and front organizations. Responses to charges of human rights violations are also attempted, indicating that external criticism on this issue has stung more than is publicly admitted. The Leninists care about what others think of them, not only for economic reasons but because international attitudes have a way of infiltrating the domestic environment in this age of the information revolution.

The third political feature of contemporary Asian Leninism that should be underlined is the leaders' obsession with stability and the belief that only through the dictatorship of the Communist Party and a reinvigoration of ideological indoctrination can stability be preserved. This concern is understandable. The collapse of Western Leninism and the attendant disorder engulfing millions of people created profound dismay. The former USSR and its satellites are privately portrayed to party members as powerful negative lessons, although the public stance is to assert that each state has the right to seek its own political and economic route. Further, without a cultural heritage of a strong civil society apart from the state, of political rights, and of individualism, the communal spirit is deeply imbedded in current Leninist elites, especially those first-generation revolutionaries who cling to power but belong to an earlier age. Finally, and perhaps most important, present leaders now realize that economic reform, however necessary, is likely to be profoundly unsettling to everyone concerned at certain points. Hence, political risks must be minimized.

Still, the central dilemma cannot be avoided. How can an old politics fit a new economics? Perhaps the mesh between these two forces was poorly effected in Gorbachev's Soviet Union. Perhaps it is dangerous to proceed with political openness if there are no economic programs in place. Nonetheless, political Leninism becomes increasingly difficult to maintain, at least in its traditional form, in a society moving toward the market at home and extensive economic intercourse with advanced democracies abroad.

5
Opportunities and Hazards in Foreign Policy

In its early years, the People's Republic of China juggled three types of relations in fashioning its foreign policy: comrade-to-comrade, people-to-people, and state-to-state.[1] On the surface at least, the deepest commitments appeared to go to comrades—not only the Soviets, but Asian comrades as well, from the North Koreans and Vietnamese to the guerrilla movements in Burma, Thailand, and Malaysia. When the break with the Soviet Union occurred, Beijing became the undisputed leader of the Asian Leninist bloc, standing against the revisionism of Khrushchev.

Today that tradition has been restored in some degree. China, North Korea, and Vietnam have banded together ideologically to proclaim to the world that whatever may happen to socialism elsewhere, they will not desert the socialist cause. Yet, as recent history shows, this alliance is precariously based. In the recent past, there was a painful interlude when Beijing decided it had to punish a naughty child (the traditional word was "bad barbarian") to its south. In the brief Sino-Vietnamese military encounter, it is not clear who taught whom a lesson, but in any case, Hanoi ultimately realized that the cost of living in a hostile relationship with its massive neighbor could only result in huge burdens; and so, jettisoning its anti-Chinese foreign minister, Nguyen Co Thach, it made amends that China graciously (and warily) accepted.

Relations with North Korea also had their unpleasant period. During the Cultural Revolution, Chinese radicals taunted Kim Il Sung, labeling him a "fat dictator who lived in luxury while his people starved." A border controversy also threatened to boil over into violence. With the end of the Cultural Revolution, however, and even more strongly after the advent of the Gorbachev era, North Korea looked to China as its only possible source of external support. For its part, China remained loyal—in its way. It gave verbal support to Kim's reunification proposal and the withdrawal of U.S. forces from the South. On ceremonial occasions, it proclaimed the relationship one of lips and teeth, sealed in the blood of the Korean War. Still, these actions only slightly inhibited the steady growth of PRC economic and cultural relations with the Republic of Korea (ROK). The DPRK remained China's legal wife, but the ROK became its favorite concubine.

It is ironic that China's greatest problems in foreign relations since the end of the Korean War have been with erstwhile comrades, first and foremost the Soviet Union. The bitter enmity that began to break into the open at the very end of the 1950s and continued until the early 1980s has now given way to "normal relations." It was in the interests of both China and Russia that a hostility costing so much in military burdens and policy inhibitions should be ended. No one ought to mistake the nature of the normalcy that now exists, however. The current Chinese leaders are profoundly displeased by political developments throughout Eastern Europe and the former Soviet Union, and they blame Mikhail Gorbachev and Boris Yeltsin for creating a disaster. The prospect of further disorder or new political movements in Central Asia, some of which might have an impact on China's border regions, is worrisome. Moreover, although economic and cultural relations have grown in recent years and will continue to expand, fundamentally there is a limit to the degree to which these two massive nations can fruitfully interact now. Both must compete in looking to the advanced industrial world for assistance, including scarce capital resources, although Russia's attention will be directed primarily to the West while that of China will be focused on the East.

Meanwhile, there are certain comrades who no longer get China's support other than in a moral sense. These are the guerrilla Marxist revolutionaries, remnants of which exist in various parts of East and South Asia. At one time, Beijing was rendering assistance in various forms to virtually all of the Asian Communist movements and to revolutionaries fighting established governments elsewhere as well. It was a costly policy, less in money than in political terms. Moreover, except in the case of Vietnam, it was a failure; and even there, the Chinese came to rue the day of Hanoi's victory.

China's people-to-people program continues, but it is now coordinated almost completely with the policy of according state-to-state relations highest priority. In essence, China has become a supporter, or at least an accepter, of the establishment, whatever it may be. It asserts its readiness to enter into relations with virtually any state on the basis of the five principles of peaceful coexistence. Only a few states like the Republic of Korea and South Africa at present remain beyond acceptability, and even these may soon be recognized. Israel was accorded recognition most recently.

Moreover, the PRC is increasingly seeking to operate as a major power. Despite repeated disclaimers of hegemonistic ambitions, China is a clear contender for regional leadership and, at a minimum, more extensive inclusion in the global decision-making process. In some degree, the end of the cold war and such events as the Tiananmen incident have reinforced the changes in Chinese foreign policy that got under way earlier, even as they have caused some tactical alterations. After the Soviet threat was perceived to have declined, in the early 1980s, the PRC shifted to a policy of nonalignment, a policy it had proclaimed during the 1960s when its attitude toward the United States and the USSR had been "a plague on both your houses." The nonalignment of the 1980s, however, was intended to be a stance friendly to both "superpowers" and to use their rivalry to China's own advantage when possible. Briefly, China had global importance in the balance of power. In reality, its stance was one of tilted alignment, and the tilt was to the United States and Japan for both economic and strategic reasons.

Under present conditions, China is much less critical on the global chessboard, although as a permanent member of the UN Security Council its voice can be heard on all global issues on which it chooses to take a stand. Still, it remains a major regional force, and one whose power may well grow with time. Not surprisingly, in recent years China has concentrated on cultivating its Asian neighbors irrespective of their political and economic structures, thereby constructing a buffer system of sorts. In addition to normalizing relations with Russia, it has wooed Japan, and with some payoff. It is pursuing a de facto two-Koreas policy. Relations with the six ASEAN states are better than ever before, with diplomatic ties reestablished with Indonesia and opened with Singapore and Brunei. At the same time, the quarrel with Vietnam has subsided; and, as one result, a precarious peace has been effected in Cambodia. Relations with Laos have improved considerably. Further to the west, China has made modest overtures to India without disturbing its close relations with Pakistan.

In sum, China's policies toward East and South Asia are more realistic and have been more successful than at any time since the founding of the People's Republic.[2] On the one hand, it has strengthened ideological ties with its few remaining Leninist neighbors, thereby giving them—and itself—some assurance that the socialist world is not completely dead. On the other hand, it has improved relations with a wide range of non-Communist Asian states, from repressive Myanmar (Burma) to the politically open countries of the region.

This is not to assert that the horizon is trouble-free. There remain a number of unresolved border and territorial issues, from that 10 percent of the border with the old Soviet Union that remains to be settled, to the issue of the Senkaku (Chiaoyutai) islands with Japan and the all-important South China Sea atolls, the subject of a long-standing controversy with Vietnam, Malaysia, the Philippines, and Taiwan.

With Taiwan, a much larger issue remains. What is to be the future of this extraordinary island and its 20 million inhab-itants—independence, de facto or de jure? That worry has steadily grown in Beijing as PRC authorities realize that time is not necessarily on their side. Will the PRC formula "one country, two systems" be achieved in some form? There is very limited support in Taiwan for such a development, given the multiple uncertainties that surround the Chinese mainland and the advent of a new generation of Taiwanese and children of mainland refugees whose personal identification with China is modest at best. The December 1991 Taiwan elections repre-sented an overwhelming defeat for the "Independence Now" forces; but contrary to some foreign observers, they did not represent a victory for the "One China" thesis. Rather, they endorsed the status quo: "De Facto Independence."

It is not surprising that despite improved relations with China, virtually every Asian neighbor has a degree of concern about the giant in their midst. Is it possible that at some point in the twenty-first century, having gotten its economic act together, China will loom up as a major power, with its "central kingdom" complex intact? The fact that the PRC has turned its attention to developing a blue-water navy does not ease this concern. Consequently, most Asian states want a U.S. strategic presence in the region, either because of a worry about China or the fear of a Japan disengaged from the U.S. connection. It is not because the United States is the most loved but because it is the least feared that this sentiment is widespread.

On the broader front, China has first of all to contend with its troubled relations with the sole remaining global power. As noted, at an earlier point China found advantage in a policy of tilted nonalignment, with the tilt toward the United States and Japan. A number of Chinese leaders would like to return to that position despite the political hazards involved. To be sure, from their standpoint the United States is a subversive force, especially in its potential influence on younger generations— its affluence, its openness, its culture are infectious. Nonetheless, there are similar risks from neighbors close at hand, and the United States is a major market, a source of technology and of investment. Moreover, excessive dependence on Japan is not desirable, even if the Japanese private sector were willing to become more involved in activities other than trade.[3]

Yet controversies with the United States seem to grow.[4] The economic issues of dumping, intellectual property protection, and prison-made goods and the question of Chinese sales of strategic weaponry have been added to the thorny problems of human rights. There is every indication that the Sino-U.S. relationship will continue to be difficult unless or until Chinese politics—and economic policies—move into a new phase. Neither government wants the relation to worsen. To the Beijing government, as noted, both economic and strategic considerations are involved. To the current Washington administration, China is important to the resolution of regional issues and too large a part of Asia to be isolated, congressional tendencies to the contrary notwithstanding.

Apart from the Pacific-Asian region, China plays a rather modest role. Its rhetorical stance is that of being a champion of the Third World, of which it considers itself a part. It costs nothing to take such a position and may have certain political advantages. Thus, periodically, Beijing calls for a more just international economic order. At the same time, China shows an interest in expanding its relations with the new European Community, hoping that this can provide an additional source of technology and investment, however modest.[5]

Contemporary China is constantly seeking to balance two images—that of a developing nation and that of a major power—the one image a reality, the other a hope. The ideological element in its foreign policy, although not wholly absent, is completely subordinate to the sense of national interest held by its leaders. Much that is traditional still motivates those leaders: an unshakable belief in China's innate superiority, hence, a high degree of self-confidence; a fierce pride that causes them to be quick to take offense when a slight is perceived; and a support for national sovereignty that is based upon nineteenth-century precepts, notwithstanding the advent of a new, interdependent world that China's leaders cannot yet comprehend.

As has been noted, the leaders of North Korea exhibit very similar traits, which may explain why the Chinese insist that they understand Korea better than anyone else. Recent global and regional developments have not been kind to the DPRK.[6] The shock to them of events in the Soviet Union can scarcely be exaggerated. Not only did Moscow destroy socialism in the West, as they view it, but it betrayed a faithful ally. To make matters more painful, North Korean spokesmen could not reveal their feelings fully in public because their dependence upon Russia, while swiftly diminishing, was still too extensive to be risked. It would take time to adjust to the new conditions governing Russian-North Korean trade and assistance.

Koreans of whatever political affiliation have never wished to be overly dependent upon China. That nation is too large, too close, and too committed to being a big brother to make an intimate Korean-Chinese relation wholly comfortable. Ties with a distant big nation and the safety that comes from a diversity of contacts are desirable, if a choice is possible. Nonetheless, the DPRK is deeply indebted to China, both for saving the regime during the Korean War and for standing by it ideologically and, to the extent possible, economically in recent times. As has been indicated, however, China has a keen sense of its national interests, and they do not fully coincide with the perceived interests of North Korea. Thus, when Beijing told the North Koreans in the spring of 1991 that they could not veto South Korea's application to enter the United Nations, Pyongyang suffered another shock.

The actions of its erstwhile major allies have forced North Korea to embark on a new foreign policy course, ending the external controversy about whether it was possible for the DPRK to change while Kim Il Sung still lived. First, the North Koreans abandoned their longtime opposition to cross-recognition by the major states and opened negotiations with Japan, looking toward diplomatic ties. Indications were also forthcoming that Pyongyang hoped to improve relations with the United States despite the unending stream of abusive propaganda. Second, the DPRK reluctantly accepted dual representation in the UN, giving up the position, also strongly held, that it would never acquiesce in the two-Koreas formula.

Most important, the North moved away from its utterly hard-line rejection of the South's overtures for a step-by-step movement toward peaceful coexistence, preliminary to unification at some future point. The first major step was the agreement to move into high-level talks, with the two prime ministers heading their respective delegations. By the end of 1991, five meetings had taken place. Although the first sessions were unproductive, the October sessions showed modest progress, and the final meeting, taking place December 11-13, resulted in what may prove to be a historic agreement entitled "Agreement on Reconciliation, Nonaggression, and Cooperation and Exchange between the North and the South."[7]

This agreement, containing 25 articles, covered the widest range of issues: noninterference in each other's internal affairs and an end to abusive propaganda; mutual nonaggression, the settlement of disputes through negotiations, and a North-South Joint Military Committee with a subcommittee to arrange for talks within one month; economic intercourse, cultural exchanges, and free travel and communications; and the creation of other joint committees to work out the details of these matters.

Even more encouraging, at the close of December it was announced that an agreement had been reached in principle for the mutual inspection of military sites in both North and South to ensure that the Korean peninsula would be nuclear-free. On January 6, 1992, President George Bush, while in Seoul, announced the conditional suspension of the joint U.S.-ROK Team Spirit exercises, and the DPRK responded immediately by announcing that it would sign the International Atomic Energy Agency (IAEA) Safeguards Agreement.

Although caution is warranted, given the numerous earlier "breakthroughs" that proved abortive, there now seems a greater prospect for tension reduction on the Korean peninsula and a wider range of cooperative measures between the two Koreas than at any other time in their 45-year existence—*if* the nuclear issue is satisfactorily resolved. What has produced this turn of events? One major factor lies in the monumental shifts in the Soviet-North Korean relationship and the important changes in Chinese policy toward the Korean peninsula with the advent of Beijing's two-Koreas policy. Certain actions by Japan and the United States are also of key importance. Japan made it clear to the North that it could not move toward diplomatic recognition until the nuclear issue was resolved and promised consultation with the ROK on matters pertaining to its Korea policy. The United States took a major step in September 1991 when President Bush announced that all U.S. tactical nuclear weapons would be removed globally, and it was made clear later that that action involved South Korea as well as other sites. President Roh Tae Woo was able to announce in December that there were no nuclear weapons in the South and to propose mutual inspection.

It can be assumed from earlier propaganda and initial responses to these measures that the rapidity of U.S. and South Korean actions caught the North by surprise, and one can guess that there were extensive discussions and debates as to the best response. To stonewall would be to block progress in relations with both Japan and the United States, the former a key to economic assistance and the latter a critical strategic concern. It would also feed the growing belief that the DPRK was seeking to develop nuclear weapons despite repeated denials by its leaders, including Kim Il Sung, that it had either the capacity or the will to do so. Some answers to the questions of North Korean nuclear capacities and intentions should be forthcoming soon.

In the present climate, North-South relations will become an ever more crucial factor in the domestic politics of both Koreas. The more immediate hazards may relate to the South. The year 1992 is a presidential election year, and there are questions as to whether the Democratic Liberal Party, the government party, can remain united. The status of the New Democratic Party, the leading opposition party, is also delicate. Should disunity become extensive, it would almost certainly affect both the pace and the nature of North-South developments. There would be an overwhelming temptation to continue with united-front politics toward the South on Pyongyang's part despite the December pledges, and there might also be a temptation among certain elements in the South apart from the radical students to make foreign policy an issue.

The unification issue has long been highly politicized in both Koreas, and in the background there has been a great deal of theater. Will that continue? Talk of an early "summit meeting" between the two presidents persists, and recent events give it greater credence. Such a meeting, if it takes place, would seem to signal Pyongyang's final willingness to accept the ROK as a political entity and would probably heighten Roh's position on the domestic political stage as well as ensure his place in history. Still, is the pledge of early unification that is likely to be emphasized in such a meeting feasible in any other than highly artificial terms at this point? A Vietnam formula (unification through force) is now ruled out by agreement. A German formula (unification by absorption) worries and angers Northern leaders, but it is also of concern to the South, given the costs and risks that would be involved. There remains the Chinese formula—which in reality is two formulas. The formal one is akin to that of the DPRK, namely, one nation, two systems. The actual formula now in effect is that of progressively increased economic and cultural interaction, with the issue of unification left to the future. Will the politics—and the economics—of North and South permit such a course?

Meanwhile, North Korean foreign policy is very likely to continue the process of enlarging contact with the market economies and, taking advantage of its position as a UN member, improving its contacts with the major nations, including the United States. If the North continues to stall on nuclear inspection, little progress on other fronts is likely; but if the nuclear issue is resolved and a process of North-South tension reduction, arms control, and economic-cultural interaction gets under way, those efforts should bear fruit. Whether this will strengthen or weaken Kim Jung Il's position when the final succession takes place can be debated, but clearly DPRK officials, including Kim Il Sung, may be gambling that young Kim's position will be strengthened by a more realistic foreign policy, whatever its hazards.

Vietnam's separation from the former Soviet Union was far less contentious than that of North Korea, but it was almost as costly in terms of the loss of military and economic assistance. Unquestionably, Moscow's decline increased Hanoi's need to mend its fences with China and to withdraw from Cambodia, as well as to compromise on the key issues involving that country that were prerequisites to such a development. Meanwhile, Vietnam demonstrated a flexibility in its relations with the non-Communist Asian states far greater than has yet been shown by North Korea, although Hanoi's recent policies may well serve as a model for Pyongyang. With promises that foreign traders and investors would be warmly greeted, Vietnam's reformers courted the private sectors of the ASEAN states, including those states less than friendly in earlier times, like Thailand and Singapore. As we have seen, performance has not generally matched promise, but the will to accommodate outsiders economically seems to be growing, especially in the south, where the bulk of investment is taking place.

The great obstacle is identified as the United States: without a lifting of the U.S. embargo, international agencies like the IMF and the World Bank are reluctant to proceed with loans, and governments like that of Japan are cautious in extending aid except on a small scale, although that country is now Vietnam's second largest trading partner, next to the former USSR. Thus, Vietnam has virtually pleaded with Washington, holding up its reformed Cambodian policies, its openness to various U.S. private groups, and its willingness to cooperate further on the thorny issue of U.S. military personnel listed as missing in action (MIA). If there are no unexpected disruptions in the peace process in Cambodia and if the reformers at least balance the hard-liners in Hanoi, changes will occur in U.S. policies, either soon or after the 1992 U.S. elections. An upgrading of official talks has already taken place, with discussions at the level of assistant secretary of state, and an agreement was reached earlier on establishing a temporary office in Hanoi, staffed by Americans, to assist in the resolution of the MIA issue.

Meanwhile, Vietnam has made it clear that it would like to have some affiliation with both ASEAN and such other regional bodies as might accept it. Its efforts to build upon relatively good relations with Indonesia to reach the other members of ASEAN are bearing some fruit, although economic conditions in Vietnam are inhibiting to most investors.

The small neighboring states of Cambodia and Laos are in the process of seeking broader contacts as well. In Cambodia, both political and economic considerations have dictated a movement by the Phnom Penh government away from Hanoi and a reaching out to the ASEAN states as well as such major nations as Japan, the United States, and China. A similar trend is to be observed in Laos, although Laotian ties with Vietnam remain extensive.

In summary, four broad trends characterize the foreign policies of the remaining Asian Leninist states. First, similar to the situation in non-Communist states, economics is in command of their international relations to an unprecedented extent. Whatever the risks, their decision has been to broaden contacts with the key market economies, looking to exports as their vehicle of development and hoping to obtain the necessary capital and technology to speed up that process. In this regard, China and Vietnam lead, but North Korea is preparing to move in a similar direction, whatever its past failures and present qualms.

Second, domestic political considerations support an ideological alliance between the trio of important Asian Leninists, despite lingering animosities between the PRC and

Vietnam. To read the speeches and literature emanating from the conservative leaderships of these societies is to realize quickly that certain themes and concepts are shared: the necessity of guarding against "peaceful evolution"; the importance of opposing Western "bourgeois liberalism"; and, above all, "the need to guard the integrity and dignity of the nation," defending socialism by proclaiming the absolute sanctity of the nation's internal affairs.

The current ideological alliance, however, is not allowed to interfere with a separate sense of national interest in each of these three states. In this respect too, trends in the Asian Leninist world are in line with those elsewhere. The nature of alliances has greatly changed. In the aftermath of the cold war, such major states or "mentors" as remain rarely make absolute commitments to the smaller or less powerful states to whom they have made pledges. All assistance is conditional. Similarly, the smaller states do not pledge absolute political obedience but reserve a goodly quotient of independence. In this sense, alliances have become alignments, with ample flexibility. So it is in the relationships among the Asian Leninists. Although each proclaims itself "nonaligned," this stance is largely fictional. No nation can be purely nonaligned in a world where economic interdependence is rife and security still hinges partially upon external relationships. Even Myanmar, a state that was probably as nonaligned as any in the world, is edging toward a series of relationships, notably with its neighbors to the north and east, that will sooner or later influence both its domestic course and its broader foreign relations.

Already, a third factor has been signaled. The Asian Leninists are participating ever more extensively in the larger process of Asianization that is taking place throughout their region. Contacts of all types between and among Asian states are steadily progressing as external influences weaken and economic necessities become the driving force. A certain tension is now building between the process of Asianization and the continuing importance within the region of the United States, a Pacific but not precisely an Asian state. In any case, as already indicated, the NETs forming throughout the region cross ideological-political boundaries, raising profound issues.

Never have domestic and foreign policies been so intertwined, constituting the single most powerful problem for the Asian Leninists.

Finally, like others, the Asian Leninists may find themselves soon without an enemy, or at least without an enemy sufficiently credible to cause their people to be willing to make heavy sacrifices in the name of preserving the nation from external attack. To some leaders, this in itself will be a frightening prospect.

6
Looking Ahead

Every generation has considered its age unique, but there are excellent reasons for the generations currently living to make that claim. At no time in previous history have the earth's inhabitants had to contend with a global revolution. The ongoing upheaval to which we are witnesses is affecting every region of the world. In such circumstances, the temptation to make sweeping generalizations is very great, and we have been treated to many of these in recent times, a few of them correct. The greatest challenge in such a period, however, is to be able to live with and make sense of complexity. There are very few simple problems or easy solutions. To an unprecedented extent, the task of leaders today is to accept these complexities and then explain them in understandable terms to the citizenry without undue distortion.

In viewing Asian communism, as with all complex phenomena, one should avoid facile explanations or confident predictions. A few guarded generalizations and an examination of some alternative scenarios, however, would seem in order. First, it is essential to understand the consequences of current economic development. Given its tempo and reach, such development brings with it three trends with profound political ramifications. First, it spawns diversity—between and within classes, among specific industrial and agrarian sectors, and also among regions of the country. A highly centralized, command economic strategy progressively betrays inefficiencies, being unable to manage the growing intricacies that stem from the developmental process.

Second, as livelihood improves, urbanization spreads, and education expands to cover a larger number of citizens, the demand for inclusiveness in the political process finds stronger voice. Fewer individuals, especially among young generations, remain satisfied with the artificial types of participation advanced under Leninism. Genuine interest groups, articulating perceived needs, emerge. A civil society apart from the state

81

gains strength. Under these conditions, the inculcation of an ideological faith is not sufficient to provide the leadership or the system with legitimacy. Performance is required. Increasingly, citizens make judgments about their government on the basis of what it is doing for them—now.

Third, development, and particularly development hinged to an ever-closer interaction with the advanced industrial world, causes societies previously closed to become porous. Autarkic economic policies doom a society to backwardness; to come abreast of contemporary science and technology it is necessary to expose oneself to a wider world. External influences from myriad sources then reach the people, even in rural areas. The historic thesis that one could borrow the hardware of development without its software is even more naive today than when it was first espoused. In sum, modernization and isolation are mutually exclusive. Distortion in the understanding of external phenomena will always be present, some of it culture-laden, and by no means confined to Leninist societies. Nonetheless, the ability of authoritarian regimes to prevent public knowledge of the outside world other than that provided by state propaganda is rapidly declining.

Taken together, these byproducts of development are rendering Leninism, at least in its traditional forms, passé. It was a technique of mass mobilization capable of being applied in specific places at specific times. Its primary purpose was to provide a framework—economic, political, and social—for rapid modernization and to remove all perceived obstacles with whatever ruthlessness was required while binding the masses to the new order through pledges of social and economic justice. It can be argued that societies that employed Leninism would have fared better had the experiment never been undertaken. Perhaps that is true, but at this point it is irrelevant. The important point is that such states are each forced to look beyond Leninism now.

Does this mean that democracy is en route to global triumph? It is interesting to recall that in the period immediately after World War II, a number of Western scholars found the theory of convergence appealing. This theory suggested, on the one hand, that liberal democracies would move in the direction of providing a range of social policies for their citizens, taking into account the needs of the least privileged, and, on the other hand, that the socialist states would broaden the political rights of their citizens, with the two systems converging in the vicinity of social democracy.

Elements of this theory have been borne out by events. Certainly, social welfare policies have spread throughout the advanced industrial world, and laissez-faire is even more out of date than Leninism. On the other hand, until very recently the hard authoritarian states of the Leninist type have resisted political change, and some still do so. More important, given differences of culture, scale, and development, there is no reason to expect political identity among the nations of the world.

Further, just as there are economic models other than the command economy or that pioneered by the United States and certain other parts of the West, so there are political models other than parliamentary democracy or Leninism.

Against this background, let us examine four possible scenarios relating to the future of Asian communism. One scenario can be labeled that of "muddling through." Under this scenario, the economic measures taken would be sufficient to produce at least minimal satisfaction among the citizenry at large, with an admixture of incentives and privatism on the one hand and extensive state ownership and control on the other. Modifications would be made in the political structure to permit a semblance of diversity, along the lines of the current policies whereby the Communist Party "listens to the voice of the people," consulting with those "parties" it has created and various other groups. Only minimal structural concessions would be made, however, and the basic Leninist political system would be maintained.

With the masses reasonably satisfied in terms of basic needs but overall economic standards remaining low, the political pressures from below could be contained. As for the intellectuals and others more cosmopolitan and sophisticated, the lines of permissibility would be carefully drawn and revised slightly when necessity dictated, but with examples periodically made of those who stepped over the line and questioned the essentials of the system. Rewards would be increased, however, for those who served socialism, including higher economic remuneration than has recently been given.

The coercive instrumentalities of the state would be kept available, and strong efforts would be made to ensure the unity of the military and security forces—first, by meeting their primary needs and desires; second, by keeping the party heavily involved in these sectors.

Obviously, this scenario is the one favored by the current Asian Leninist leaders, and they define their efforts in this direction as "socialism with (Chinese, Korean, Vietnamese) characteristics." Elements of Asian tradition—particularly communalism—render assistance. Moreover, economic growth that is perceptible but modest and the genuine fear of chaos under alternative scenarios can or do provide additional support. Yet, as suggested, the dynamics of economic development and the interdependence of societies stemming from the present phase of the scientific-technological revolution will render the "muddling through" scenario very difficult to sustain over a protracted period of time.

At the opposite end of the spectrum of possibilities is a scenario that can be labeled the "big bang" scenario. Under it, the Leninist states would undergo explosive upheavals and disintegration in one form or another. China, for example, would divide in a manner similar to the Soviet Union, with various independent or quasi-independent regions. Perhaps developments would be more tumultuous, with a return to warlordism and chaos. North Korea would undergo the fate of East Germany, being absorbed by the South after a rapid post-Kim Il Sung disintegration. Vietnam would become ungovernable, and political division might again ensue.

This scenario with suitable variations cannot be ruled out, at least in one or two cases, and it is the specter of chaos upon which Leninist leaders play in seeking to hold the loyalty of their people. Such a scenario will require at least two prior conditions, however: continuing economic failures of significant magnitude and an extensive breakdown of unity among the political and military elites. There is virtually no capacity for a revolt from below in these societies at this point. From this source, the far more likely development is cynicism and indifference, which are occurring in China and Vietnam. Disintegration, therefore, would hinge on protracted elitist disunity—warring at the top, as it were, and the breakup of centralized control.

A third scenario, and that desired by liberals and not a few intellectual dissidents within several of the Asian Leninist states, is that of a rapid transition to political pluralism and an open society. They cling to the hope that with Leninism in the West moving in that direction, and with democracy making progress in other parts of Asia as well as elsewhere in the Third World, this is a feasible goal.

Although this scenario cannot be dismissed as totally impossible, it does not seem likely at present. It is not wholly accidental that Leninism has survived in three Asian states. The historic legacy that they bear, combined with their stage of economic development and geopolitical circumstances, has sustained a hard authoritarian system, now subject to increasing pressures. To move to parliamentary democracy in the near term, unless through a process of absorption, would be to enter an enormously difficult political arena with few if any of the prerequisites for success.

It should not be forgotten that at the end of World War II, a number of ex-colonies in Asia and elsewhere turned to parliamentarism because it had been the political system of their colonial masters. Only in cases where the indigenous elites had been extensively tutored by those masters did democracy survive, and even in those cases the democratic path has been a precarious one—for example, in India. There has been no such tutelage in China, North Korea, or even Vietnam. (The French, unlike the British, did not transmit their political values—perhaps because they were so divided in the pre-1945 period about what those values were.) There are new generations of cosmopolitan intellectuals emerging in some of these societies, as has been noted, a portion of whose members seem prepared to carry the banners of democracy, but they are still few in number and weak in power. It must never be forgotten that these are societies where the vast countryside, with its peasant masses, hangs over the urban areas like a canopy, affecting politics as well as other aspects of society. Unfortunately, with the exception of China, where rigorous measures have been pursued, rural birth rates are alarmingly high, ensuring that this condition will continue. Only the most determined optimist among liberals can believe that democracy lies immediately ahead for Asia's Leninist states.

One interesting fact, however, should not be overlooked. In some countries of Asia, parliamentarism has been combined with a dominant party system, ensuring stability while permitting a significant degree of political openness. Note the case of Japan. Although political pluralism exists in that nation and the requisite freedoms to make choice meaningful are fully in operation, national power has not alternated between parties for more than 40 years. The dominant party system has its merits for developing societies, but as Japan itself illustrates, it does not encourage optimal responsibility on the part of either those who govern or those who oppose. Nevertheless, it is a system that attracts many Asians because it appears to enable a combination of stability and development.

The political record of modern Asia, including that of Asia's current parliamentary democracies, suggests a fourth scenario for the remaining Leninist states, a scenario that I have labeled "authoritarian pluralism."[1] Under this scenario, political change would be greater than in the case of "muddling through," but considerably less than that required for genuine democracy. Political choice would be constrained, whether by law or by fact; and political freedoms relating to speech, publication, and assemblage would be limited, although the limits would be vague, constantly shifting and continuously tested.

Apart from the state, however, a civil society would emerge and grow, demonstrating resilience even when put under pressure by anxious political authorities. Thus, in fields like education and religion, considerable autonomy would exist, and a diversity of ideas would emerge. In the economic realm, moreover, privatism and the market would play critical roles, although the state would be a crucial actor, employing neomercantilist policies.

Authoritarian pluralism is the route that was earlier followed by South Korea and Taiwan among others. One of its characteristics is that it does not pretend to be the ultimate system, but only a stage in the evolutionary progression. Soft authoritarian leaders, indeed, generally insist that when conditions are ripe, they—or their successors—will expand the arena of freedom. The reluctance to give up power, to be sure, sometimes makes the progression uneven and on occasion fraught with violence. Still, the ideological and structural rigidity of utopian systems like Leninism is lacking.

Among the four scenarios outlined above, none can be dismissed as totally impossible, and it is conceivable that the three Asian Communist states will take different courses in the future. If one were to construct a table of probability, however, the authoritarian-pluralist scenario would seem to be the most likely future for these societies, at least in the short term.

Irrespective of the course pursued, one can be certain that the problems of relating to an increasingly interdependent world will be very serious. Consequently, for the Asian Communists, nationalism will be an instrument of rising importance. A supreme irony of this period is that the remaining Leninists, once the champions of the brotherhood of the global proletariat and the unity of the socialist world, are now using nationalism as their main line of defense, whereas the liberal democracies, from whence nationalism in its modern form sprang, are being dragged, however reluctantly, toward internationalism out of economic necessity.

Nationalism, to be sure, is a powerful force in most nations today, including the advanced industrial West. Indeed, in some respects it is resurgent, because in an age of ideological decline it is a substitute of sorts in rallying citizens to meet new types of perceived threats. Certainly, the United States is not immune to this trend. Economic nationalism seems destined to advance in America as in Europe. Nonetheless, as was noted earlier, there is a nineteenth-century quality to the manner in which nationalism is currently featured in Asia's Leninist states. The nation-state is treated as if its sovereignty were absolute, and most types of external influence or involvement are defined as "interference" and forms of aggression.

Still, even the Leninists are beginning to appreciate that when a state's domestic policies impinge heavily upon those with whom it has extensive economic contact, such policies are no longer a purely domestic matter. Chinese leaders, for example, are not unaware of the Structural Impediments Initiative talks between the United States and Japan, where many aspects of each nation's structure as well as its policies have been subject to examination. On a more restricted basis, Chinese leaders have accepted economic negotiations with one of their major market outlets, the United States.

Similarly, the thesis that human rights, however these are defined, are the exclusive prerogative of the nation immediately concerned is denied by the United Nations Charter, to which all of these states are signatories, and, more important, by the political realities of this age. What a state does to its people now reverberates throughout the world, helping to shape public attitudes elsewhere and, hence, to affect policies. The task of internationalizing human rights issues so that they are not merely the reflection of a single culture is vital and is still in a preliminary stage. Nonetheless, drawing the remaining Leninist states into this process has begun and will continue.

If one rejects a theory of lineal progression and avoids the simplistic view that the world is headed toward a utopian future of freedom, prosperity, and peace, there is much reason for cautious optimism, including optimism about the way in which certain states will evolve beyond Leninism.

Global war is less likely than at any other time in the twentieth century, and despite the fact that we have certainly not seen the end of domestic and regional violence, the opportunity to reduce armaments is rapidly improving. This opportunity could make a great difference in the developmental potentials of desperately poor countries, including those in the Leninist category.

Meanwhile, science and technology continue to make the type of advances that can speed up the developmental process remarkably, assuming correct economic and social policies are found and followed. Despite the barriers to change that have been noted, it is becoming increasingly clear that many Leninist mistakes of the past can be remedied even if the short-term pain is intense.

Further, if, as seems likely, the political spectrum is narrowed with both traditional monarchies and hard authoritarian systems of the Leninist type forced to change significantly, the capacity for interchanges of all types across political lines will be enhanced.

These facts argue strongly for nations like the United States to pursue policies that avoid seeking to isolate the Asian Leninist societies. Greater interaction with others is a powerful agent for change, especially in authoritarian states. For the remaining Leninist societies, this is a transitional period in every sense; and the transition can be influenced by widening contacts, unofficial and official.

It is not necessary to hide the issues between us, nor to avoid rigorous negotiations. It is necessary to remember that none of these states is completely monolithic at present. Whatever validity the term "totalitarianism" had in the past (and its defect was that it assumed a degree of reach and control that no government ever attained), it is no longer applicable, even to a society like North Korea. Let us accept that fact in formulating our attitudes and policies toward the besieged Leninist strongholds.

Notes

Chapter 1 — The Background

1. This statement is taken from Kh. Choibalsan, *Speeches and Articles*, vol. 1, p. 141, as quoted in *Socialist Mongolia*, trans. Nadezhda Burova and Kathleen Cook (Ulaanbataar: State Publishing House of the Mongolian People's Republic, 1981), 23.

Chapter 2 — The Consolidation of Power

1. For an on-the-scene account by a talented observer of the period just preceding the Communist victory and the initial period of Communist control, see A. Doak Barnett, *China on the Eve of Communist Takeover* (New York: Praeger, 1963). A relatively early evaluation of Chinese rule by a number of young American scholars can be found in A. Doak Barnett, ed., *Chinese Communist Politics in Action* (Seattle: University of Washington Press, 1969). For a more recent analysis, see essays in Roderick MacFarquhar and John K. Fairbank, eds., *The Cambridge History of China*, vol. 14, *The People's Republic of China, Pt.1, The Emergence of Revolutionary China, 1949–1965* (Cambridge: Cambridge University Press, 1988).

2. A penetrating analysis of the setting of the Cultural Revolution is Roderick MacFarquhar's *Origins of the Cultural Revolution,* 2 vols. (London: Oxford University Press, 1974; New York: Columbia University, 1983).

3. A detailed account of the early years of the Korean Communists is found in Dae-Sook Suh, *The Korean Communist Movement—1918–1948* (Princeton: Princeton University Press, 1967) and Robert A. Scalapino and Chong-Sik Lee, *Communism in Korea,* vol. 1, *The Movement* and vol. 2, *The Society* (Berkeley: University of California Press, 1972).

4. For a scholarly study of the background of Vietnamese communism, see Huynh Kim Khanh, *Vietnamese Communism 1925–1945* (Ithaca, N.Y.: Cornell University Press, 1982).

5. Consult Bernard Fall, *The Two Vietnams—A Political and Military Analysis* (New York: Praeger, 1968); Donald

Lancaster, *Emancipation of French Indochina* (London: Oxford University Press, 1961); Phillippe Devillers, *Histoire du Vietnam de 1940 à 1952* (Paris: Editions du Seuil, 1952); William J. Duiker, *The Communist Road to Power in Vietnam* (Boulder, Colo.: Westview Press, 1981); Douglas Pike, *History of Vietnamese Communism, 1925–1976* (Stanford: Hoover Institution Press, 1978) and *PAVN: People's Army of Vietnam* (Novato, Calif.: Presidio Press, 1986); Robert F. Turner, *Vietnamese Communism—Its Origins and Development* (Stanford: Hoover Institution Press, 1975); and Peter Braestrup, ed., *Vietnam as History* (Washington, D.C.: University Press of America, 1984).

6. For a well-documented study of modern Cambodia, see David P. Chandler, *The Tragedy of Cambodian History— Politics, War, and Revolution since 1945* (New Haven: Yale University Press, 1991). Many Americans are familiar with Christopher Hudson's novel *The Killing Fields* (New York: Dell Publishers, 1984), generally through the motion picture version.

7. See Joseph J. Zasloff and Paul F. Langer, *North Vietnam and the Pathet Lao—Partners in the Struggle for Laos* (Cambridge: Harvard University Press, 1970).

8. Three significant works on recent trends in Chinese ideology and politics that should be consulted are Andrew Nathan, *Chinese Democracy* (New York: Knopf, 1985); Lowell Dittmer, *China's Continuous Revolution* (Berkeley: University of California Press, 1987); and Hong Yung Lee, *From Revolutionary Cadres to Bureaucratic Technocrats in Socialist China* (Berkeley: University of California Press, 1990).

9. The title of one of the many biographies of Kim Il Sung provides an example of the idolization: O Tae Sok, Paek Bong, and Li Sang Gyu, *The Benevolent Sun,* 2 vols. (Pyongyang: Foreign Languages Publishing House, 1980).

10. For example, see Vietnamese Communist Party General Secretary Do Muoi's speech of October 22, 1991, to the meeting of the Ho Chi Minh City party congress. *Nhan Dan* (Hanoi), October 23, 1991, pp. 1, 3, reproduced in Foreign Broadcast Information Service (henceforth FBIS) East Asia (henceforth EAS), November 21, 1991, pp. 50–59.

Chapter 3 — The Economic Challenge

1. On economic developments in the first years, urban and rural, see T. J. Hughes and D.E.T. Luard, *The Economic Development of Communist China 1949–1958* (London: Oxford University Press, 1959). For a PRC interpretation, see Hsueh Mu-chiao, Su Hsing, and Lin Tse-Li, *The Socialist Transformation of the National Economy in China* (Peking: Foreign Languages Press, 1960).

2. Two fine works dealing with agrarian conditions in the PRC after the Deng-sponsored reforms are William L. Parish, ed., *Chinese Rural Development: The Great Transformation* (Armonk, N.Y.: M. E. Sharpe, 1985) and Jean C. Oi, *State and Peasant in Contemporary China* (Berkeley: University of California Press, 1989).

3. See Nicholas R. Lardy, *China's Entry into the World Economy* (Lanham, Md.: University Press of America, 1987); Carl Riskin, *China's Political Economy* (New York: Oxford University Press, 1987); Wei Lin and Arnold Chao, *China's Economic Reforms* (Philadelphia: University of Pennsylvania Press, 1982); Dorothy J. Solinger, ed., *Three Visions of Chinese Socialism* (Boulder, Colo.: Westview Press, 1984); James A. Dorn and Wang Xi, eds., *Economic Reform in China— Problems and Prospects* (Chicago: University of Chicago Press, 1990); and Robert Kleinberg, *China's "Opening" To The Outside World* (Boulder, Colo.: Westview Press, 1990). In Chinese, see Ma Hong and Sun Shangqing, eds., *Zhongguo Jingji Jiegou Wenti Yanjiu* (Research on problems of China's economic structure), 2 vols. (Beijing; Renmin Chubanshe, 1983).

4. Among many sources, read Elizabeth J. Perry and Christine Wang, *The Political Economy of Reform in Post-Mao China* (Cambridge: Harvard University Press, 1991); Niu Genying, "An Economy Regulated by a Combination of Plans and Market Force," *Beijing Review,* October 7–13, 1991, pp. 17–21; Song Yi, "Changes in China's Agriculture," *Beijing Review,* October 7–13, 1991; Nicholas R. Lardy, "Economic Reform in China" (Paper prepared for the Asia Society U.S.-Japan Consultative Group on China, New York, December 18–19, 1991); Jorgen Delman, Clemens Stubbe Ostergaard, and Flemming Christiansen, eds., *Remaking Peasant China*

(Aarhus, Denmark: Aarhus University Press, 1990). For two
Japanese views, see Kazuo Yamanouchi, "The Chinese
Economy—An Overview," JETRO *China Newsletter,* January–
February 1991, pp. 2–7, 23, and Kyoichi Ishihara, "The Post-
NPC Chinese Economy—Present State and Outlook," JETRO
China Newsletter July–August 1991, pp. 8–15.

5. Consult Denis Fred Simon and Merle Goldman, eds.,
Science and Technology in Post-Mao China (Cambridge:
Harvard University Council on East Asian Studies, 1989), and
Li Cheng and Lynn T. White III, "China's Technocratic Move-
ment and the *World Economic Herald,"* *Modern China* (July
1991): 342–388. For a Chinese view on future training, see
Zhai Feng, "Upgrade China's Labour Force," *China Daily* (New
York), November 9, 1991, p. 4.

6. See Wang Xiangwei, "Soaring Growth Prompts Warn-
ing," *China Daily* (New York), November 9, 1991, p. 2.

7. A series of excellent papers on recent economic and
political developments in the PRC is contained in Richard
Baum, ed., *Reform and Reaction in Post-Mao China—The
Road to Tiananmen* (New York: Routledge, 1991). See also the
article by Barry Naughton, "The Chinese Economy: On the
Road to Recovery?" in William A. Joseph, ed., *China Briefing
1991* (Boulder, Colo: Westview Press, 1992).

8. A succinct overview is Hang-Sheng Cheng, *Lessons
From China's Economic Instability, 1979–1990,* Issue Paper
(San Francisco: The 1990s Institute, 1991).

9. For a report of the five-day "working conference" held
in Beijing September 23–27, 1991, and an analysis of the
problems and proposed solutions, see the English *Xinhua*
(Beijing) report carried in FBIS-China (CHI), September 27,
1991, pp. 37–38. Also read an article by Willy Wo-lap Lam,
South China Morning Post (Hong Kong), September 24, 1991,
p. l, carried in FBIS-CHI, September 27, 1991, pp. 38–39.

10. See Robert A. Scalapino, "The United States and Asia:
Future Prospects," *Foreign Affairs* 70, no. 5 (Winter 1991/92):
19–40.

11. Two additional works of significance are Constance
Squires Meaney, *Stability and the Industrial Elite in China
and the Soviet Union* (Berkeley: Institute of East Asian Stud-

ies, 1988), and Wang Zhuo, "The Principal Contradiction in Integrating the Planned Economy with Regulation Through Market Mechanism," original in *Jingji Yanjiu* (Beijing), August 20, 1991, pp. 60–62, reproduced in FBIS-CHI, October 10, 1991, pp. 41–44.

12. Ye Dexu and Tian Huiming, "Dai Yuanchen Looks Forward to China's Economy in the 1990s," *Zhongguo Xinwen She* (Beijing), January 22, 1991, in FBIS-CHI, January 30, 1991, pp. 41–42.

13. Li Peng, "Report on the Outline of the Ten-Year Program and of the Eighth Five-Year Plan for National Economic and Social Development" (Speech delivered at the fourth session of the Seventh National People's Congress, March 25, 1991), *Beijing Review,* April 15–21, 1991, pp. 1–24; also in FBIS-CHI, June 14, 1991, pp. 1–24; also Jiang Zemin's Speech on the occasion of the tenth anniversary of the founding of the Chinese Communist Party, July 1, 1991, reproduced in FBIS-CHI, July 5, 1991, pp. 1–14.

14. For background, in addition to works cited, consult Joseph S. Chung, *The North Korean Economy: Structure and Development* (Stanford: Hoover Institution Press, 1974) and "Economic Planning in North Korea" in Robert A. Scalapino and Jun-Yop Kim, eds., *North Korea Today—Strategic and Domestic Issues* (Berkeley: Center for Korean Studies, Institute of East Asian Studies, 1983). See also Park Choon-Sam, "The Self-Reliance Efforts of the North Korean Economy," parts I, II, *Vantage Point* (October, November 1991): 1–10, 1–11.

15. On the investments by Koreans affiliated with *Chongryun,* the pro-North Korean General Federation of Koreans in Japan, see a report from Radio Beijing, contained in *North Korea News* (Seoul), October 21, 1991, pp. 4–5.

16. Several interesting accounts are Karoly Fender (former official of the Hungarian Foreign Ministry), "Economic Problems of the Democratic People's Republic of Korea in the 1980s," (Paper prepared for an international seminar in Taipei, June 24, 1991), reproduced in *Information Service on the Unification Question of the Korean Peninsula,* publication of the National Unification Board, Republic of Korea,

February 25, 1991, pp. 31–42; and Il-Dong Koh, "Complementarity of Industrial Structures Between North and South Korea" (Paper prepared for a conference sponsored by the Institute of East Asian Studies—East-West Center—Korean Association for the Study of Socialist Societies [henceforth IEAS-KASSS], Berkeley, Calif., December 11–13, 1991).

17. On North Korean trade and debt, also see *Korea Herald* (New York), March 16, 1991, p. 8; Jung Chang Young, "North Korea's Trade Policy," IEAS-KASSS Conference.

18. The recommendations of the United Nations Development Program regarding the North Korean economy for 1992–1996 are summarized in FBIS-EAS, July 31, 1991, pp. 21–22.

19. An overview is presented by Toshio Watanabe, "North Korea's Worst Enemy Is Still Itself," *Asian Wall Street Journal Weekly,* January 14, 1991, p. 1. See also Rhee Sang-Woo, "North Korea in 1991: Struggle to Save Chuch'e Amid Signs of Change," *Asian Survey* 32, no. 1 (January 1992).

20. Personal observations by the author, May 1991.

21. For comparative data, in addition to Koh, "Complementarity of Industrial Structures" and other citations, see Hacheong Yeon, "Prospects for North-South Korean Economic Relations and the Evolving Role of Korea in Northeast Asian Economic Development" (Seoul: Korea Development Institute, 1991).

22. On the peasant markets, see an article entitled "News From North Korea," *Kyonghyang Sinmun* (Seoul), November 11, 1991, p. 9, published in FBIS-EAS, November 20, 1991, pp. 22–23.

23. On the first direct North-South trade, see *North Korea News* (Seoul), August 5, 1991, pp. 3–4. Also "Pyongyang Requests Quick Delivery of South Korean Rice," *North Korea News* (Seoul), August 5, 1991, pp. 1–2.

24. See *Choson Ilbo* (Seoul), March 19, 1991, p. 19, published in FBIS-EAS, March 20, 1991, pp. 24–25.

25. On the joint venture bank, see, among other sources, *North Korea News* (Seoul), December 2, 1991, pp. 3–4.

26. See Hajime Izumi, "Prospects for North Korean Participation in the Regional Economy," and Sung-Hoon Kim, "Prospects for Regional Economic Cooperation in Northeast Asia:

The Republic of Korea's Perspective," both papers for the
IEAS-KASS Conference.

27. A detailed analysis of the CPV Sixth Congress is given
in Gerhard Will, *Der 6. Parteitag der KP Vietnams: Aufbruch
zu neuen Ufern?* (The sixth rally of the Vietnam Communist
party: Departure for new shores? summary in English) (Cologne: Bundesinstituts für ostwissenschaftliche und
internationale Studien, December 1987). On all aspects of
contemporary Indochina, the *Indochina Chronology,* a quarterly publication of the Institute of East Asian Studies, Berkeley, Calif., edited by Douglas Pike, is very valuable.

28. See Osamu Nariai and Osamu Suruga, *The Survival
Game in Vietnam: Coping with the Consequences of Eco-
nomic Reform,* Policy Paper (Tokyo: International Institute for
Global Peace, June 1990) and Osamu Nariai, *Paths of Reform
in Vietnam,* Policy Paper (Tokyo: International Institute for
Global Peace, March 1991). Another very useful survey is Yozo
Tanaka and Keiichiro Izumi, "An Outlook on Vietnam's
Economy and Investment Opportunities," *Rim* (Mitsui Re-
search Institute, Center for Pacific Business Studies) 4, no. 10
(1990): 4–13.

29. See Brian van Arkadie, ed., *Report on the Economy of
Vietnam* (New York: United Nations Development Program,
1990). For an overview of the situation in 1990 and 1991, see
Douglas Pike, "Vietnam in 1990—The Last Picture Show,"
Asian Survey 31, no. 1 (January 1991): 79–86, and "Vietnam
in 1991—The Turning Point," *Asian Survey* 32, no. 1 (January
1992); see also Charles Joiner, "The Vietnam Communist
Party Strives to Remain the 'Only Force,' " *Asian Survey* 30,
no. 11 (November 1990): 1053–1065, and a paper by
Tetsusaburo Kimura, "Where is Vietnam Heading?" (Tokyo:
Research Institute for Peace and Security-East Asian Security
Institute Conference on Indochina, May 15–18, 1990). The
official statistics on Vietnam's trade and economy are contained in *Trade of Vietnam: 1986–1990* (Hanoi: Ministry of
Trade, Statistical Office, 1991).

30. On the population problem, see "Vietnam—Hard
Times Ahead," *Asia Pacific Briefing Paper,* no. 4 (Honolulu:
East-West Center, 1991).

31. On the CPV Seventh Congress, the following documents are essential: Vo Chi Cong's opening remarks, FBIS-EAS, June 26, 1991, pp. 13–15, and Nguyen Van Linh's *Political Report,* FBIS-EAS Supplement, June 26, 1991, pp. 15–28.

32. Pham Minh, "The Difficulties Are Severe, But There is a Way Out," *Quan Doi Nhan Dan* (Hanoi), March 31, 1991, pp. 1, 4, in Joint Publication Research Service-Southeast Asia (henceforth JPRS-SEA), May 31, 1991, pp. 46–47.

33. Nguyen Van Linh, *Political Report,* 16.

34. For two interpretations, see Nayan Chanda, "Winning the Peace—South's Reformers Gain in Vietnamese Cabinet," *Asian Wall Street Journal Weekly,* August 19, 1991, pp. 1, 18; Gwen Robinson, "New Vietnam premier seen as reformer," *Nikkei Weekly* (Tokyo), August 17, 1991, p. 20.

35. See Susumu Awanohara, "Handicapping Hanoi—U.S. Hurdle to Vietnam's IMF/World Bank Ties," *Far Eastern Economic Review* (Hong Kong), October 17, 1991, pp. 13–14; and "Weighing up Vietnam," *Economist,* October 19, 1991, pp. 35–36. An Australian view is to be found in Ron Scherer, "Australian Business Sees Vietnam's Hidden Charm," *Christian Science Monitor,* November 27, 1991, p. 6. For the experiences of Korean companies in Vietnam, see an article by Paek Sung-hun in *Tong-A Ilbo* (Seoul), March 25, 1991, p. 7, reproduced in FBIS-EAS, March 26, 1991, pp. 26–27.

36. For Heng Samrin's report, reported in *Samleng Pracheachon* (Phnom Penh), October 17, 1991, see FBIS-EAS, October 18, 1991, pp. 29–33.

37. For a candid appraisal, see Kawi Chongkittawon, "Raking Profits From the Gulf War," *Nation* (Bangkok), February 6, 1991, p. A8, in JPRS-SEA, March 14, 1991, p. 3. Five journalists have provided excellent reports and analyses of the Cambodian situation in the recent past: Chongkittawon in the *Nation* (Bangkok), Jacques Bekaert for the *Bangkok Post,* Nayan Chanda for the *Asian Wall Street Journal,* and Murray Hiebert and Susumu Awanohara for the *Far Eastern Economic Review* (Hong Kong).

38. For the Fifth Party Congress of the Laotian People's Revolutionary Party, including documents, see FBIS-EAS Supplement, April 12, 1991.

39. A report of the deputy head of the agriculture and forestry service of Luang Prabang Province, Vientiane Radio Network, December 4, 1991, reported in FBIS-EAS, December 4, 1991, p. 47. See also "Laos: Poor but Positioned for Profit," *Asia Pacific Briefing Paper,* no. 11 (Honolulu: East-West Center, 1991).

40. Two articles dealing with Mongolian economic reforms are Susan Carey, "Free From Moscow, Mongolia Makes Up For Lost Time by Embracing Markets," *Wall Street Journal,* August 4, 1991, p. 4; and William L. Valenti, "Mongolia Deserves Aid in Restructuring," *Asian Wall Street Journal Weekly,* July 8, 1991, p. 12. For a broad survey of developments during 1990, see William R. Heaton, "Mongolia in 1990—Upheaval, Reform, but No Revolution Yet," *Asian Survey* 31, no. 1 (January 1991): 50–56.

41. See also the July 1 report of Prime Minister D. Byambasuren, given in FBIS-EAS, July 3, 1991, p. 11.

42. A report on this poll is carried in *Montsame* (Ulaanbataar), June 28, 1991, published in FBIS-EAS Supplement, July 3, 1991, p. 13.

Chapter 4 — The Quest for Stability

1. Li Peng, "Report on the Outline," FBIS-CHI, June 14, 1991, pp. 1–24.

2. Jiang Zemin, Speech, FBIS-CHI, July 5, 1991, p. 4.

3. A pioneering study of China's minorities is June Teufel Dreyer, *China's Forty Million: Minority Nationalities and National Integration in the People's Republic of China* (Cambridge: Harvard University Press, 1976). On the issue of minority unrest, see Thomas Heberer, *Droht dem Chinesischen Reich der Zerfall? Bedrohung durch wachsende Nationalitätenunruhen* (Does disintegration menace the Chinese empire? The threat from growing unrest among national groups; summary in English) (Cologne: Bundesinstituts für ostwissenschaftliche und internationale Studien, 1991).

4. Among the many fine studies of the Tiananmen incident and its aftermath, see Tang Tsou, "The Tiananmen Tragedy: The State-Society Relationship, Choices, and Mechanisms in

Historical Perspective," in Brantly Womack, ed., *Contemporary Chinese Politics in Historical Perspective* (Cambridge: Cambridge University Press, 1991), 265–327. For the perspective of a liberal Chinese journalist, see Yi Mu and Mark V. Thompson, *Crisis At Tiananmen—Reform and Reality in Modern China* (San Francisco: China Books, 1989).

5. Jiang Zemin, Speech, 1–2.

6. Ibid., 6–7.

7. Ibid., 11.

8. Ibid., 11–13.

9. Information Office of the State Council, *Human Rights in China* (Beijing, November 1991).

10. See Parris H. Chang, *The Rule of Old Men in China: Policy Issues and Prospects for the Future* (New York: The Asia Society, July 1991). Two stimulating general studies of Chinese politics are Lucian Pye, *The Mandarin and the Cadre: Chinese Culture* (Ann Arbor: Center for Chinese Studies, University of Michigan, 1988) and Vivienne Shue, *The Reach of the State: Sketches of the Chinese Body Politic* (Stanford: Stanford University Press, 1988). For two excellent articles dealing with China's judicial system, see Margaret Y. K. Woo, "Adjudication Supervision and Judicial Independence in the P.R.C.," *American Journal of Comparative Law* 39 (Winter 1991): 95–119, and "Legal Reforms in the Aftermath of Tiananmen Square," *Review of Socialist Law,* no. 1 (1991): 51–74.

11. On the CCP and the military, for two earlier studies, see Ellis Joffe, *Civil-Military Relations—Chinese Defense Policy* (Urbana: University of Illinois Press, 1984) and Monte Bullard, *China's Political-Military Evolution—The Party and the Military in the PRC, 1960–1984* (Boulder, Colo.: Westview Press, 1985). Recent items of interest include Harlan W. Jencks, "Party Authority and Military Power: Communist China's Continuing Crisis," *Issues and Studies* (Taipei) (July 1990): 11–39, and an unpublished paper by Feng Shengbao, "Party and Army in Chinese Politics: Neither Alliance Nor Opposition." One should also read Deng Xiaoping, "The Army Should Subordinate Itself to the General Interest, Which is to Develop the Country" (Speech delivered on November 1, 1984) (Beijing: Foreign Language Press, 1987).

12. For two insightful articles, see David Shambaugh, "China in 1991—The Year of Living Cautiously," *Asian Survey* 32, no. 1 (January 1992), as well as his earlier essay, "China in 1990—The Year of Damage Control," *Asian Survey* 31, no. 1 (January 1991): 36–49.

13. In addition to the works cited, consult Chong-Sik Lee, *Korean Workers' Party* (Stanford: Hoover Institution Press, 1978); Young Whan Kihl, *Politics and Policies in Divided Korea: Regimes in Contest* (Boulder, Colo.: Westview Press, 1984); C. I. Eugene Kim and B. C. Koh, eds., *Journey to North Korea—Personal Perceptions* (Berkeley: Institute of East Asian Studies, 1983); and Robert A. Scalapino and Dalchoong Kim, eds., *Asian Communism—Continuity and Transition* (Berkeley: Institute of East Asian Studies, 1988).

14. These figures come from the DPRK Central Broadcasting Station, as reported in *North Korea News* (Seoul), no. 607, p. 6.

15. For an eulogistic account of Kim Jung Il, see Choe In Su, *Kim Jong Il—The People's Leader,* 2 vols. (Pyongyang: Foreign Languages Publishing House, 1983, 1985).

16. One interpretation of the current political scene can be found in the article by Rhee Sang-Woo, "North Korea in 1991," previously cited.

17. An excellent illustration of these three themes is to be found in an editorial in *Nodong Sinmun* (Pyongyang) entitled "Let Us Further Glorify the Popular Masses-Centered Socialism of Our Own Style, Following the Party's Banner," October 10, 1991, reproduced in FBIS-EAS, October 16, 1991, pp. 23–28.

18. Kim Jung Il, *Our Socialism Centered on the Masses Shall Not Perish* (Pyongyang: Foreign Language Press, 1991).

19. Ibid.

20. Ibid., 16–17.

21. Nguyen Van Linh, *Political Report,* 21.

22. Ibid.

23. Ibid.

24. Kim Phung, interview with Bui Tin, published in *Que Me* (Paris), January–February 1991, pp. 17–28, excerpted in JPRS-SEA, April 26, 1991, pp. 30–35.

25. Ibid., 32.

26. Ibid., 35. Bui Tin asserted that he had great respect for President Ho, having had a personal relationship with him. He added that Ho's teachings were now 20 years old, however, and were Ho alive, he would change. He added, "If I said this in Vietnam, they would accuse me of talking nonsense, because these [Ho's views] are regarded as sacred and immutable dogmas."

27. Among the U.S.-based organizations that have been watching human rights violations in Vietnam are Asia Watch; the Aurora Foundation (see *Violations of Human Rights in the Socialist Republic of Vietnam—April 1975–December 1988,* Atherton, Calif., 1989); *Vietnam Update,* published quarterly by the Institute for Democracy in Vietnam, Washington, D.C.; and *Indochina Journal,* Burlingame, Calif.

28. For a complete listing of those elected to the CPV Politburo (13), Secretariat (9), Control Commission (9), and Central Committee (146), see FBIS-EAS Supplement, July 2, 1991, pp. 16–18.

29. One interesting insight into party-military relations is provided by an editorial in *Quan Doi Nhan Dan* (Hanoi), September 2, 1991, pp. 1, 4, reproduced in FBIS-EAS, September 24, 1991, pp. 57–58. See also Nguyen Tri Dung, "Renovation in Teaching Marxism at Army Institute," excerpted in FBIS-EAS, October 11, 1991, pp. 68–70.

30. A timely, insightful article is that by Douglas Pike, "Vietnam in 1991—The Turning Point."

31. Party political platform, presented by Heng Samrin, October 17, 1991, in FBIS-EAS, October 18, 1991, p. 30.

32. Ibid.

33. For background studies on the Cambodian political scene, see Frederick Z. Brown, *Cambodia and the Dilemmas of U.S. Policy* (New York: Council on Foreign Relations, 1991); Jusuf Wanandi, *The Cambodian Conflict,* Special Report (Tokyo: International Institute for Global Peace, January 1990); and *1991: A Critical Year for Indochina* (Tokyo: Report of Pacific Basin Studies Program and Research Institute for Peace and Security, March 1991). Current appraisals include Frederick Z. Brown, "Cambodia in 1991—An Uncertain Peace," *Asian Survey* 32, no. 1 (January 1992); Kawi

Chongkittawon, "Hun Sen-Chea Sim Alliance on a Rocky Path?" *Nation* (Bangkok), October 9, 1991, p. A10, reproduced in FBIS-EAS, October 10, 1991, pp. 29–30; and a report on the new "French-style" constitution in *Nation* (Bangkok), November 13, 1991, p. A4, reproduced in FBIS-EAS, November 13, 1991, p. 42.

34. The revised Lao People's Revolutionary Party (LPRP) rules and regulations, as enacted at the Fifth Party Congress in Vientiane, March 28, 1991, are reprinted from *Pasason,* the party organ, in FBIS-EAS Supplement, April 12, 1991, a special issue devoted to coverage of the congress. The Laotian judicial system and criminal code are presented in another special issue, JPRS-SEA, March 4, 1991. A current analysis is Stephen T. Johnson, "Laos in 1991—Year of Challenge," *Asian Survey* 32, no. 1 (January 1992).

Chapter 5 — Opportunities and Hazards in Foreign Policy

1. For general studies relating to Chinese foreign policy, see A. Doak Barnett, *China and the Major Powers in East Asia* (Washington, D.C.: Brookings Institution, 1977) and *The Making of Foreign Policy in China: Structure and Process* (Boulder, Colo.: Westview Press, 1985); Harry Harding, ed., *China's Foreign Relations in the 1980s* (New Haven: Yale University Press, 1986); Peter Van Ness, *Revolution and Chinese Foreign Policy* (Berkeley: University of California Press, 1970); Harold C. Hinton, *China's Turbulent Quest: An Analysis of China's Foreign Relations since 1949,* rev. ed. (New York: Macmillan, 1972); Samuel Kim, *The Third World in Chinese World Policy* (Princeton, N.J.: Center of International Studies, Princeton University, 1989); Samuel Kim, ed., *China and the World: Chinese Foreign Policy in the Post-Mao Era,* rev. ed. (Boulder, Colo.: Westview Press, 1989); Lillian G. Harris, *China's Foreign Policy toward the Third World* (New York: Praeger, 1985); Gerald Segal, ed., *The China Factor: Peking and the Superpowers* (New York: Holmes & Meier, 1982); Yufan Hao and Guocang Huan, eds., *The Chinese View of the World* (New York: Pantheon Books, 1989); Harish Kapur, ed., *As China Sees the World* (London: Frances Pinter, 1987);

Zhao Quansheng, "Domestic Factors of Chinese Foreign Policy: From Vertical to Horizontal Authoritarianism," in Allen Whiting, ed., *Chinese Foreign Policy, Annals of the American Academy of Political and Social Science* (January 1992): 159–176.

2. For elaboration of these points, see Robert A. Scalapino, "China's Foreign Policy: Coming of Age," in Joyce K. Kallgren, ed., *Building a Nation-State—China after Forty Years* (Berkeley: Institute of East Asian Studies, 1990), 1–40.

3. A fine study on recent Sino-Japanese relations is Allen S. Whiting, *China Faces Japan* (Berkeley: University of California Press, 1989).

4. Among the many works on recent PRC-U.S. relations, see Michel Oksenberg, "The China Problem," *Foreign Affairs* 70, no. 3 (Summer 1991): 1–16; Robert G. Sutter, "Tiananmen's Lingering Fallout on Sino-American Relations," *Current History* (September 1991): 247–250; and Scalapino, "The United States and Asia—Future Prospects." For PRC perspectives, read Pan Tongwen, "New World Order—According to Mr. Bush," *Beijing Review,* October 28–November 1, 1991, pp. 12–14, and Xi Runchang, "Collapse of the Post-War Bipolar Pattern and its Impact on the World," *Foreign Affairs Journal* (Beijing) (December 1990): 1–9.

5. For Li Peng's comments on China's relations with Europe, see his interview with an Italian journalist, "Li Peng on China's Foreign Relations," in *Beijing Review,* September 23–29, 1991, pp. 11–14.

6. In addition to works already cited, recent studies of DPRK foreign policy include Jae-kyu Park, Byung-chul Koh, and Tae-hwan Kwan, eds., *The Foreign Relations of North Korea: New Perspectives* (Seoul: Westview Press-Kyungnam University Press, 1987) and the following papers prepared for the IEAS-KASSS Conference, December 11–13, 1991: Larry A. Niksch, "The Two Koreas and the Major Powers"; Chae-Jin Lee, "U.S. and Japanese Policies Toward Korea"; Li Changhuan, "China and the Korean Peninsula: A Personal View"; and B. C. Koh, "Foreign Policy Implications of Domestic Political Developments in the Two Koreas." See also Kim Il Sung's interview with the director of the Japanese press, Iwanami Shoten,

published in *Sekai* (Tokyo), September 26, 1991, and excerpted in a press release by the DPRK UN mission, New York, November 13, 1991.

7. The agreement of December 13, 1991, has been reproduced in various places, among them, *Korea Update,* Embassy of the Republic of Korea, Washington, D.C., December 16, 1991.

Chapter 6 — Looking Ahead

1. Robert A. Scalapino, *The Politics of Development: Perspectives on Twentieth-Century Asia* (Cambridge: Harvard University Press, 1989).